JONATHAN SWIFT

Macmillan Literary Lives
General Editor: Richard Dutton, Reader in English,
University of Lancaster

This series offers stimulating accounts of the literary careers of the most widely read British and Irish authors. Volumes follow the outline of writers' working lives, not in the spirit of traditional biography, but aiming to trace the professional, publishing and social contexts which shaped their writing. The role and status of 'the author' as the creator of literary texts is a vexed issue in current critical theory, where a variety of social, linguistic and psychological approaches have challenged the old concentration on writers as specially gifted individuals. Yet reports of the 'death of the author' in literary studies are (as Mark Twain said of a premature obituary) an exaggeration. This series aims to demonstrate how an understanding of writers' careers can promote, for students and general readers alike, a more informed historical reading of their works.

Published titles

WILLIAM SHAKESPEARE *Richard Dutton*
JONATHAN SWIFT *Joseph McMinn*
PERCY BYSSHE SHELLEY *Michael O'Neill*
JOHN DONNE *George Parfitt*
ALEXANDER POPE *Felicity Rosslyn*
JOSEPH CONRAD *Cedric Watts*
CHARLOTTE AND EMILY BRONTË *Tom Winnifrith and Edward Chitham*
D. H. LAWRENCE *John Worthen*

Forthcoming titles

JAMES JOYCE *Morris Beja*
JOHN MILTON *Cedric Brown*
GEORGE ORWELL *Peter Davison*
JANE AUSTEN *Jan Fergus*
THOMAS HARDY *James Gibson*
HENRY JAMES *Kenneth Graham*
JOHN DRYDEN *Paul Hammond*
WILLIAM WORDSWORTH *Keith Hanley*
BEN JONSON *David Kay*
W. B. YEATS *Alastair MacRae*
GEORGE ELIOT *Kerry McSweeney*
VIRGINIA WOOLF *John Mepham*
ALFRED, LORD TENNYSON *Leonee Ormond*
JOHN KEATS *David B. Pirie*
T. S. ELIOT *A. E. Sharpe*
GEOFFREY CHAUCER *Barry Windeatt*
EDMUND SPENSER *Gary W*

Series Standing Or

If you would like to receive future titles in this series as they
are published, you can make use of our standing order
facility. To place a standing order please contact your
bookseller or, in case of difficulty, write to us at the address
below with your name and address and the name of the
series. Please state with which title you wish to begin your
standing order. (If you live outside the UK we may not have
the rights for your area, in which case we will forward your
order to the publisher concerned.)

Standing Order Service, Macmillan Distribution Ltd,
Houndmills, Basingstoke, Hampshire, RG21 2XS, England.

Jonathan Swift

A Literary Life

Joseph McMinn
Lecturer, Department of English
University of Ulster at Jordanstown

MACMILLAN

First published 1991

Published by
MACMILLAN ACADEMIC AND PROFESSIONAL LTD
Houndmills, Basingstoke, Hampshire RG21 2XS
and London
Companies and representatives
throughout the world

Printed in Hong Kong

British Library Cataloguing in Publication Data
McMinn, Joseph
Jonathan Swift. — (Macmillan literary lives).
1. English literature. Swift, Jonathan, 1667–1745
I. Title
828.509

ISBN 0–333–48584-X (hardcover)
ISBN 0–333–48585–8 (paperback)

For Edna

Contents

Preface, with Suggestions for Further Reading

The guiding emphasis of the following narrative is that of a career and a life devoted to writing. This excludes textual interpretation and comprehensive biographical detail whenever such factors do not bear on Swift's practice as poet, pamphleteer and correspondent. Steering between literary criticism and a biographical history, I have tried to present an account of Swift's formation and development as a writer. Occasionally, such a pure course is impossible, given the historical character of Swift's status as a writer. For example, since politics and friendship play such a central role in his literary career, some contextual information is necessary if the coherence of the narrative is to be sustained.

A literary life, therefore, tries to give imaginative attention to the practice and process of writing. One of the constant tensions in Swift's career is that between his self-image as a principled amateur and the emergent commercialisation of his trade. Printers and publishers are crucial to that career. Swift's ambivalent resistance to the literary market-place is partly reflected by a love of anonymity and pseudonymity (he hardly ever signed his name to anything he wrote) and by the large number of writings he withheld from publication. Also, his duty and outlook as a clergyman should never be ignored or underestimated in trying to appreciate the zeal and consistency of his public writings: the material welfare of his Church provided one of his favourite literary pulpits. Yet he rarely wrote well when defending his own views: the most testing contradiction in his writings is that between the radical style of his assault on others and the uncomplicated conservatism of his personal values. Swift discriminated very emphatically between different kinds of writing and audiences, especially between public and private work, or 'literary' and 'necessary' publications. In studying his career, we must enlarge our understanding of the very term 'literature'.

Anyone writing about Swift's career has no excuse for being poorly armed. The canon of his writings is a magisterial achievement. This consists of *The Prose Works of Jonathan Swift*, edited by H. Davis, 14 vols (Oxford, 1939–68); H. Williams' edition of *The*

Journal to Stella, 2 vols (Oxford, 1948), which has been added to
Davis as Vols XV and XVI, and completes the set; *The Poems of
Jonathan Swift*, edited by H. Williams, 3 vols, 2nd edn rev.
(Oxford, 1958) (a handier and, in many details, more up-to-date text is
Jonathan Swift: The Complete Poems, edited by Pat Rogers (London,
1983)); *The Correspondence of Jonathan Swift*, edited by H. Williams, 5
vols (Oxford, 1963–5), (Vols IV and V now partially revised by
D. Woolley, 1972). In my notes, these three editions are abbrevi-
ated as *PW*, *Poems*, and *Corr*. An authoritative, fully annotated
selection of Swift's main writings may be read, conveniently, in
Jonathan Swift, The Oxford Authors Series, edited by Angus Ross
and David Woolley (Oxford, 1984).

For comprehensive information on editions of Swift, see
H. Teerink, *A Bibliography of the Writings of Jonathan Swift* (1937, 2nd
edn rev., A. H. Scouten, Philadelphia, 1963). The most up-to-date
review of Swift scholarship is *Swift Studies – 1965–1980: An
Annotated Bibliography*, by R. Rodino (New York, 1984). There is
now a *Supplemental Bibliography of Swift Studies 1965–1980*, by
R. Rodino, H. Real and H. Vienken, published in *Swift Studies*, 1987,
Universität Münster. Such journals are the best source for keeping
abreast of Swift scholarship and of pursuing specialist interests in
this large field. Three other valuable journals deserve note: *Eighteenth-Century Ireland*, *Eighteenth-Century Studies*, and *The Scrible-
rians*.

My own narrative would have been impossible without the
resources and arguments opened up by other critics and biog-
raphers. Foremost amongst these, inevitably, is Irvin Ehrenpreis,
whose *Swift: The Man, His Works, and The Age*, 3 vols (London,
1962–83), displays an eloquent synthesis of all scholarly skills.
Shorter, more specialised biographies worth consultation are
J. Downie, *Jonathan Swift: Political Writer* (London, 1984), and
D. Nokes, *Jonathan Swift: A Hypocrite Reversed* (Oxford, 1985). An
excellent book, the only full-length one of its kind, is O. Ferguson,
Jonathan Swift and Ireland (Urbana, Ill., 1962). The standard historical
work on Swift as clergyman is L. Landa, *Swift and the Church of
Ireland* (Oxford, 1954). A superb interdisciplinary study which
applies contemporary literary theory with precision and power, is
C. Fabricant's *Swift's Landscape* (Baltimore and London, 1982).

I would like to thank Andrew Carpenter for initial inspiration;
Richard Dutton, my editor, for efficient and regular advice; Her-
mann Real, for inviting me to speak on the subject at Münster;

Ronnie Bailie, for having read the draft-text with his usual scrupulousness; and Janet Campbell, a typist to beat them all. My wife has endured all this, with understanding and humour, longer than anyone: such friendship helped finish the work, and I thank her above all.

J. MCMINN

1
Secretary and Apprentice

The strongest influences on the young Jonathan Swift were religious and legal rather than literary: clergymen and public servants stand out as models of personal and public ambition.[1] In his unfinished autobiographical sketch, *Family of Swift*, written when he was almost sixty, Swift singled out his grandfather, Thomas, as a worthy example of commitment and achievement.[2] In Swift's tribute, the Royalist parson's political loyalty to the Crown and his material self-sacrifice are the outstanding virtues in a life based on integrity, but one which ended without recognition of his public service. The only literary figure in Swift's family tree was John Dryden, a second cousin once removed, on his father's side. Although he liked to point out this kinship, there is no question of literary influence. Swift's father, Jonathan, after emigrating from England in 1660, worked in the King's Inns in Dublin, but died shortly before his son's birth in November 1667. Two of Swift's uncles, Godwin and William, became solicitors in Dublin, while a third, Adam, became an MP for County Down. A fourth uncle, Thomas, stayed in England and became a clergyman. The young Swift was raised and educated by his Uncle Godwin, now a successful attorney attached to the great Ormonde family in Kilkenny. All of these newly arrived immigrants, filled with ambition after the Restoration, had done quite well for themselves in a land which promised many opportunities for loyal Protestants within its legal and religious system. None of them is associated with a literary interest.

Although Swift asserted that, by the age of three, 'he could read any chapter in the Bible',[3] the evidence of his days at school and university hardly suggests a prodigy or a latent genius. On the contrary, the record is quite unexceptional. Kilkenny School, the best of its kind in Ireland, was Uncle Godwin's choice for his young nephew. Swift's widowed mother, seeing that her son was now financially secure, returned to her home in Leicester. At school, the curriculum was strict and conservative, most of it through the medium of Latin. As with all forms of education at the

1

time, religion was central to the training received. Kilkenny School stood for the promotion of Anglican doctrine and morality.[4] The only close friend Swift seems to have had at school was his cousin Thomas, son of Uncle Thomas, the clergyman.

Both cousins entered Trinity College Dublin in April 1682, when Jonathan was fifteen years old. The clerical character of the University was as fundamental as Kilkenny, and most graduates went on to become Anglican clergymen. Apart from developing a close friendship and life-long regard for his tutor, St George Ashe, a member of the Dublin Philosophical Society, Swift's time at Trinity seemed no more than a necessary formality which ended in minor humiliation. After nearly seven years of formal schooling in the classics and rhetoric, he was awarded his BA under special regulations. As the elderly Dean, speaking in the third person, he later recalled this anti-climax with some irritation:

> . . . and when the time came for taking his degree of batchelor, although he had lived with great regularity and due observance of the statutes, he was stopped of his degree for dullness and insufficiency, and at last hardly admitted in a manner little to his credit, which is called in that college *speciali gratia*. And this discreditable mark, I am told, stands upon record in their college registry.[5]

By the beginning of 1689, because of the war between William of Orange and King James, most of the staff and students at Trinity left for the safety of England. Swift, now aged twenty-one, took advantage of the move to find his first job. The young graduate with his new, slightly devalued degree, went back to his mother in Leicester, and secured a post which signalled the beginning of his literary ambition.

In the summer of 1689, with King William on the throne, and the 'Glorious Revolution' nearly complete, Swift took up the post of personal secretary to Sir William Temple, an ex-diplomat living in prosperous retirement at Moor Park in Surrey. This post was secured through a former friendship between Swift's parents and Temple's father, and seems to have been a small favour by the distinguished Temple to the fatherless son of a respectable family. Swift later wrote that 'he was received by Sir William Temple, whose Father had been a great Friend to the Family'. After only a year in his first job, Swift decided to return to Ireland, being told by physicians that his dizzy spells (later known as Ménières disease, which was to afflict him for the rest of his life) might be cured by a more familiar climate. Our first picture of Swift as secretary comes in a letter of May 1690 which Temple wrote to a friend, Sir Robert Southwell, then Secretary of State for Ireland, to see if another post could be found for the young man:

> . . . I venture to make you the offer of a servant, in case you may have occasion for such a one as this bearer. He was borne and bred there (though of a good family in Herefordshire) was neer seven years in the Colledge of Dublyn, and ready to take his degree of Master of Arts, when he was forced away by the desertion of that Colledge upon the calamitys of the Country. Since that time he has lived in my house, read to mee, writ for mee, and kept all accounts as far as my small occasions required. He has latine and greeke some French, writes a very good and current hand, is very honest and diligent, and has good friends though they have for the present lost their fortunes in Ireland and his whole family having been long known to mee obliged mee thus farr to take care of Him.[6]

Swift's company may have been polite, but he was clearly a literary menial. His Irish birthplace did not seem to help and, in the letter of reference, is immediately qualified by his solidly English heritage. He was a statesman's literary companion at this stage, but only 'as far as . . . small occasions required'. Temple tried to use his influence to secure the young secretary a post as 'a gentleman to wait on you, or as a Clarke to write under you'. On a more academic note, he even suggested Southwell could find Swift a vacant fellowship at Trinity. The letter is not very enthusiastic, no fellowship was found, and Swift returned to Moor Park the following year. At Temple's household, Swift made the acquaintance of a young, teenage girl, Esther Johnson, daughter of a servant-family. 'Stella' later became Swift's closest, lifelong friend, and a most intimate source of literary inspiration.

Swift's literary career began with poetry rather than prose. His first serious efforts at imaginative literature began shortly after his return to Moor Park, and consisted of a series of solemn Odes.[7] Between the summers of 1690 and 1691, the young secretary, now aged twenty-three, composed 'Ode to the King', an inflated panegyric on King William. In it he praises the new monarch's political and civic virtues in a style both pompously formal and rhythmically dull. Consciously imitating the 'grave' style of Abraham Cowley's Pindaric Odes, Swift then wrote a second poem, 'Ode to the Athenian Society', and posted it to the learned society of that name, hoping it would be published in their journal. The poem and the accompanying letter were promptly published, and Swift saw himself in print for the first time. Like many of the early poems, this Ode conceals the youth of its author through the adoption of a stylistic gravity probably more suited to Temple than his secretary. Yet Swift also tries to adapt the form to his innocence:

> Pardon Ye great Unknown, and far-exalted Men,
> The wild excursions of a youthful pen:
> Forgive a young and (almost) Virgin-muse,
> Whom blind and eager Curiosity
> (Yet Curiosity they say,
> Is in her Sex a Crime needs no excuse)
> Has forc't to grope her uncouth way
> After a mighty Light that leads her wandring Eye.[8]

Neither enthusiasm nor honesty redeems the tedium of the verse, whose formal demands, felt here in the nervous and apologetic parentheses, place too great a strain on the budding versifier.

In his correspondence of this period, we get a fresher and more dramatic picture of Swift's literary apprenticeship. Writing to Rev. John Kendall, a friend at Leicester, he says that '. . . in these seven weeks I have been here, I have writt, & burnt and writt again, upon almost all manner of subjects, more perhaps than any man in England'.[9] Hyperbole of this kind is the most characteristic motif in the verse: in the correspondence, however, it enlivens rather than detracts from the style. Writing to his cousin, Thomas, his most intimate and youthful correspondent at this time, he swaps notes about the creative grind:

It makes me mad to hear you talk of making a Copy of verses next morning, which tho indeed they are not so correct as yr others are what I could not do under 2 or 3 days, nor does it enter my head to make any thing of a sudden but what I find to be exceeding silly stuff except by a great chance, I esteem the time of studying Poetry to be 2 hours in a morning, and that only when the humour sits, which I esteem for the flower of the whole Day, and truly I make bold to employ them that way and yet I seldom write about 2 Stanzas in a week I mean such as are to any Pindarick Ode, and yet I have known my self in so good a humour as to make 2 in a day, but it may be no more in a week after, and when all's done, I alter them a hundred times, and yet I do not believe my self to be a laborious dry writer, because if the fitt comes not immediately I never heed it but think of something else, and besides, the poem I writt to the Athen. Society was all ruff drawn in a week, and finished in 2 days after, and yet it consists of 12 stanza [sic] and some of them above thirty lines . . .[10]

Swift clearly took his early verse very, even too, seriously. In most of the verse, he tends to express himself in a style which might suggest a maturity desired but not yet achieved. The letters to his cousin, however, are playful and spontaneous, as is to be expected from two relatives who are not long out of college and trying to become successful and respectable young men in the world. Swift could even confess his own artistic egotism to Thomas:

> . . . and I have a sort of vanity, or Foibles, I do not know what to call it, and which I would fain know if you partake of it, it is (not to be circumstantiall) that I am overfond of my own writings. I would not have had the world think so for a million, but it is so, and I find when I writt what pleases me I am Cowley to my self and can read it a hundred times over . . .[11]

Swift wrote two more Odes: one on his master, William Temple, the other on Dr William Sancroft, the Archbishop of Canterbury who defied both King James and King William in defence of the Established Church. Both heroes exemplify Swift's early admiration for principled conservatism. He is also attracted to his retirement from the world of corrupt politics:

> And divine SANCROFT, weary with the weight
> Of a declining Church, by Faction her worse foe opprest,
> Finding the Mitre almost grown
> A load as heavy as the Crown,
> Wisely retreated to his heavenly rest.[12]

Although this sympathy with world-weariness seems slightly incongruous coming from a poet in his twenties, Swift was never to forget these images of unrewarded virtue.

Swift is not yet an accomplished poet, but several features of this portentous verse are of lasting interest. The poems are exercises in moral character, hence the allegorical and abstract nature of the style. There is no narrative element in their execution. Also, as Ehrenpreis points out, none of their attitudes is ironic.[13] A series of solemn tributes to outstanding individuals unmoved by popular or common emotion, they are literary aspirations towards civic principle. Swift's sense of humour and economy have yet to emerge.

We should remember, however, that Swift's verse was entirely incidental to his post as Temple's secretary. He still had ambitions, and it was unclear whether his prospects would be accelerated or hampered by his residency on the Surrey estate, doing literary odd-jobs for a retired diplomat. Swift had gone up to Oxford in July 1692 to receive his MA, but was still unsettled about his career. At the end of that same year, he wrote to his uncle William, thanking him for a reference sent to Oxford. In this letter, dated 29 November 1692, we hear for the first time Swift's frustration with his job and the probability that he will become a clergyman:

> I am not to take orders till the King gives me a Prebendary: and Sir William Temple, tho' he promises me the certainty of it, yet is less forward than I could wish; because, I suppose he believes I shall leave him, and upon some accounts, he thinks me a little necessary to him . . .[14]

One of Swift's last duties for Temple seemed to promise the influence and contacts he must have envied in his master. While the Triennial Act was being debated amongst English politicians, an Act which would require the Commons to be summoned at least once every three years (a change to which King William was opposed), Swift was sent directly to the King to present Temple's argument in support of a bill to introduce the Act. As a secretary, he spent most of the time in Court, and spoke briefly to the Monarch. The bill failed.[15] Nearly half a century later, Swift wrote icily, 'This was the first time that Mr Swift had any converse with Courts, and he told his friends it was the first incident that helped to cure him of vanity.'[16] It is also clear that Swift, unlike his master, did not support a bill which would lessen the King's authority and force him to compromise with a faction over the power of parliament.

In the spring of 1694, Swift decided he had had enough of Moor Park, and that he would enter the Church. From his mother's house in Leicester, on the way back to Ireland, he wrote to another cousin, Deane Swift, relaying the scene with Temple before leaving Moor Park: 'He was extream angry I left Him, and yet would not oblige Himself any further than upon my good Behaviour, nor would promise any thing firmly to Me at all; so that every Body judged I did best to leave Him.'[17] After nearly five years service, including the temporary absence in Ireland for reasons of health, Swift was only promised a basic reference. But he had decided, as he later put it, to choose a clerical career 'without being driven into the Church for a maintenance',[18] and seemed quite determined about leaving his angry and seemingly ungrateful patron.

To his mortification, Swift was told by the Archbishop of Dublin, Narcissus Marsh, that a full and detailed reference was required from Temple before ordination could be considered. In the only letter he ever wrote to Temple, nervous but respectful, Swift politely requested a fair but prompt reference. The reason for this requirement must have dismayed Swift, who explained to Temple:

> ... that after so long a standing at the University, it is admired I have not entered upon something or other (above half the Clergy in this Town being my Juniors) and that it being so many Years since I left this Kingdom, they could not admit me to the Ministry without some Certificate of my Behaviour where I lived.[19]

Now almost twenty-eight years old, Swift's residence in England seemed like an absence or a fault to be justified. But he had no choice: 'the Sense I am in, how low I am fallen in Your Honour's Thoughts, has denied Me Assurance enough to beg this Favour till I find it impossible to avoyd.'[20] Asking Temple, politely, to hurry up, required tact and style. The prescribed date for ordination lay three weeks away. To Swift's surprise and relief, Temple replied immediately: he was ordained deacon at the end of October, and in January 1695 became a priest in the Church of Ireland.

Swift now seemed settled in an independent but humble career as a mature novice in the Church. Almost thirty, he was beginning his apprenticeship in a new system of bureaucracy which required certain duties and services before promotion could be considered. Two weeks after ordination, he was presented to his first living, the prebend of Kilroot in County Antrim, about twenty miles from Belfast in the diocese of Down and Connor. This was an overwhelmingly Presbyterian area, with very few Anglicans, and must have seemed a grim beginning after service with a famous English diplomat.[21] He was free but friendless.

Soon, however, he got to know some of the local gentry and families of Carrickfergus and Belfast, and thereby met his first romantic love. Only one letter survives from his year in Kilroot, an unusual piece by Swift's ironic standards. This is a love-letter and marriage proposal to Jane Waring, who resided in Belfast, and was nicknamed 'Varina' by Swift.[22] After the usual sentimental effusions, the priest-lover delivers an ultimatum: if she accepts him, he will stay in Ireland; if not, she will never see him again. She had two weeks to decide, then his ship would sail. With an eye on Temple's request to return, he writes, 'I am once more offered the advantage to have the same acquaintance with greatness that I formerly enjoyed, and with better prospect of interest.' Jane, little wonder, did not reply to this imperious letter and Swift was soon back at Moor Park where he began.

Outwardly, this pattern seems like a regression, a failure to advance either a clerical or a literary career. Yet this pattern of restless migration conceals one of the great literary mysteries of Swift's artistic achievement. Most commentators now agree that *A Tale Of A Tub*, his first major satire, was secretly begun in the isolation of Kilroot.[23] The consensus is that Swift, once away from the demands of Temple, had the time, inspiration and hidden talent to write this extraordinary work. Some critics even accept the story by Deane Swift that the *Tale* was begun when Swift was a student at Trinity, and that the manuscript was seen by several persons, when its author was barely twenty.[24] The argument for Kilroot is more convincing, however, especially since the emergent satire against religious dissent and fanaticism was being composed in a place notorious for such zeal. Once back at Moor Park, Swift completed the work in secrecy, and it was eventually published in 1704, anonymously.

If we accept this pattern of part-time composition over many years, then we are faced with an extraordinary case of the split character of Swift's creative process. Most of his writing up to 1700 is dutiful, with little evidence of outstanding literary talent or even ambition. Yet all the time Swift must have been privately playing with the outline of his first satirical extravaganza. Part of the reason for this secrecy is that Temple would not have approved of such literary radicalism,[25] and Swift was quite content to use his more conventional talents to suit his patron's requirements, since this kind of service, however joyless, was a training and a discipline which might result in important contacts for the future.

Swift's playful and intimate literary correspondence with his cousin, Thomas, also provides a clue to the early composition of the *Tale*. He had left a copy of part of the work with his cousin, who acted as resident chaplain to Temple while Swift was in Kilroot. Thomas had then publicised the strange work to several people. It was even rumoured that Thomas, not Jonathan, was the real author.[26] When the fifth edition of the *Tale* appeared in 1710, Swift still pointed to Thomas as the 'leak' in the anonymous arrangement, and wrote to his publisher:

> I cannot but think that little Parson-cousin of mine is at the bottom of this, for, having lent him a copy of some part of, &c, and he shewing it, after I had gone for Ireland, and the thing abroad, he affected to talk suspiciously, as if he had some share in it.[27]

At every stage in the planning, composition and reception of the text, Swift wished to remain private and anonymous. That so great a literary talent is never indicated by his minor work at this stage is not necessarily a contradiction. It is, as we will see later, a strategy prompted by practical caution. There were some things more important than literary fame or notoriety. The last thing the young clergyman wanted, on returning to Moor Park for the third time, was evidence of an outrageous imagination.

When he returned to Surrey in 1696, Swift had two immediate concerns. The first was to cut all clerical ties with Kilroot, and transfer his property to England; the other was to act as editor for Temple's vast collection of personal writings. He had arranged a replacement at Kilroot, the Rev. John Winder, with whom he maintained a close friendship. Swift's worry was to get his own library sent safely across the Irish Sea: 'I would have you send me a List of my Books, and desire you will not transmitt them to Dublin till you gett all together: I will not pardon you the loss of any.'[28] After several months, his books started to arrive, but Swift wrote again to tell Winder to keep those books not worth sending. In this second letter, dated 13 January 1699, we hear him exercising a degree of self-censorship on his juvenalia, especially his early sermons and love-letters:

> The sermons You have thought fitt to transcribe will utterly disgrace You, unless you have so much credit that whatever comes from You will pass: They were what I was firmly resolved to burn and especially some of them the idlest trifling stuff that ever was writt, calculated for a Church without a company or a roof; like our [Chapel at] Oxford; they will be a perfect lampoon upon me . . .
> I remember those Letters to Elisa, they were writt in my Youth. You might have held them up and no body of my friends would have opend them: Pray burn them.[29]

Now aged thirty-one, Swift sounds embarrassed at the thought of his clerical and romantic scribblings. It is interesting that he never felt the same about his early poetry, despite its solemnity and obscurity. Also, it is clear that Swift was already very selective about what kinds of writing he wished to be associated with, or considered of public interest. Sermons and letters were usually excluded from his idea of 'literature'.[30] From the beginning of his literary career, Swift drew a clear distinction between private writing and public literature: one was for pleasure or necessity, the other for instruction and entertainment.

His immediate professional concern at Moor Park was to transcribe, edit and publish Temple's writings. Swift now seemed to rank higher in Temple's view than previously, and was entrusted with the literary reputation of one of England's best-known statesmen. Temple's writings consisted mainly of diplomatic memoirs and personal letters. Much work on this material had already been done by a former secretary, but Swift's job as editor and amanuensis was to finish the process and see it through to publication. Editing the material also required Swift's skills as a translator of French and Latin, often the languages of international diplomacy.

Temple died in 1699, and Swift published two volumes of Temple's *Letters* in London the following year, the *Miscellanea* in 1701, a third volume of *Letters* in 1703, and, finally, the *Memoirs* in 1709. He took advantage of his editorial position to personally dedicate the *Letters* to King William, and to write a preface in which he pays tribute to people in high places. This was no time for shyness or anonymity. In the preface, he commends the stylistic and dramatic value of the letters as a unique form of writing, in which 'one may discover, the Character of most of those Persons, he writes to, from the Stile of his Letters'.[31] This was soon to prove true of Swift himself.

Once Temple died, Swift was soon out of work. A measure of his responsibility and trust at Moor Park is evidenced by the duties he had to perform to settle Temple's personal affairs.[32] He paid off legacies and bills, bought funeral clothes for the family, and paid the fee for Temple's burial in Westminster Abbey. He also advised Esther Johnson and her guardian, Rebecca Dingley, to settle in Ireland, where their legacy from Temple would better ensure their security. Swift himself now had to look for a new post. After some fruitless efforts at soliciting favours from the Court, he eventually agreed to act as chaplain and private secretary to the Earl of Berkeley, who was travelling to Ireland to take up his new post as a Lord Justice. They left for Ireland in August 1699. Ten years of secretarial service ended with the renewal of an old discipline.

While serving Lord Berkeley as private secretary, Swift was appointed as vicar to the small parish of Laracor in County Meath, a parish about thirty miles north-west of Dublin. This new living was also quite close to the Berkeley mansion in Chapelizod, on the outskirts of the city. For three years there is no surviving correspondence, and we do not know much about Swift's literary activity during this period. However, it is clear that he was continuing to work on *A Tale Of A Tub*, and was completing his first political pamphlet, *Contests and Dissensions between the Nobles and the Commons in Athens and Rome*, which was both written and published in 1701. The antithetical character of these two texts shows yet again Swift's ability to suit his style to any occasion and to an extraordinary variety of issues. Yet both texts share a common purpose. They were written in response to contemporary controversies in religion and politics and, most obviously in the case of the *Contests and Dissensions*, were used by Swift to advance his reputation as a moderate and articulate churchman. Swift's ambition was controlled by caution: both texts, the pamphlet and the satire, were published anonymously.

We should also note that Swift looked to England, never Ireland, as the proper centre of literary ambition. For the vicar of Laracor, advancement was ultimately controlled by powers in London. If he was to escape from Ireland and secure prestige and influence, he would have to attract attention to himself. In 1701, a major political debate which threatened constitutional stability took place in England. Four Whig ministers had been impeached by the House of Commons, at the instigation of the Tories, over issues of diplomatic corruption. Swift immediately saw an opportunity to declare his loyalties and, at the same time, to make important contacts with powerful men. The impeachments were soon dropped, but Swift ensured that his pamphlet was published after the issue which prompted it, thus seeming wise after the event.

Contests and Dissensions is a political allegory using classical examples of tyranny to warn the present of the dangers of repeating history. Strategically arranging correspondences between victims of ancient tyranny and the possible fate of the Whig ministers, Swift warned against the danger of submitting to any form of factional discontent. The pamphlet is supremely conservative and traditional in its view of the proper balance of powers within the State. Calculated to please and impress, it succeeded perfectly in what it intended to achieve. It was widely read and approved, and, all legal dangers past, its author now acknowledged responsibility for his tribute to Whig statesmanship. All this was a piece of literary diplomacy which would have pleased Temple, whose sober style is evident throughout the magisterial pamphlet. Swift came to know the Whig minister, Lord Somers (to whom he would dedicate *A Tale Of A Tub* three years later), and even enjoyed a short audience with the King.

Being secretary to a Lord Justice had several practical advantages for Swift, since Berkeley regularly visited London on business. Travelling with him, Swift could oversee publication of Temple's writings, keep in touch with current debate, and establish literary and political contacts. Most importantly, as with the *Tale*, it allowed him to understand the literary value of timing the publication of controversial work. Visits to London, and the success of his first political pamphlet, seem to have delighted Swift, and gave him a new sense of importance. Writing in December 1703 to the Rev. William Tisdall, a friend in Dublin, at the height of yet another controversy about legal toleration for non-conformists, he says, 'I would be glad to know men's thoughts of it in Ireland; for myself, I am much at a loss, though I was mightily urged by some great people to publish my opinion.'[33] After a display of name-dropping, including the Bishop of Salisbury and 'my Lord Somers', he concludes defiantly, 'I shall return in two months, in spite of my heart. I have here the best friends in nature, only want that little circumstance of favour and power.' Now aged thirty-six, Swift was beginning to feel that a worthy and secure career as clergyman and writer in England was there for the taking. All the while carrying with him the manuscript of the *Tale*, he decided that the satire on fanaticism would ensure the reward he so anxiously and nervously desired.

In the spring of 1704, an anonymous volume appeared in London containing three satires – *A Tale Of A Tub*, *The Battle Of The Books*, and *The Mechanical Operation Of The Spirit*. It was published by John Nutt who, three years previously, had printed *Contests and Dissensions*. Swift's involvement in the first printing of the *Tale* was deliberately obscured in order to distance himself from any immediate controversy. Not for the last time in his writing career, he published anonymously for tactical rather than principled reasons. The satirical volume was instantly popular and commercially successful, and went into two further editions in its first year. A fourth edition appeared in 1705. By then, the *Tale* had generated enough debate and argument over its authorship and meaning to decide Swift that a defence and an explanation were in his own interests. He approached another publisher, Benjamin Tooke, who had worked with Swift on Temple's *Miscellanea* in 1701, and prepared what is now taken to be a 'definitive' fifth edition to the enigmatic work. This edition appeared in 1710, still anonymous, but with a lengthy 'Apology' at the beginning of the volume, and with a host of explanatory footnotes and marginal comments. The mysteries of dating, sources, authorship and intention, which had arisen over the previous six years, were only partially resolved by this witty and impatient 'Apology'.

The confident and aggressive tone of the 'Apology' gives us a rare opportunity to listen to Swift generalise about his literary taste and purpose without the added subterfuge of a fictional mask. Even though the three satires have very specific historical targets, they are the result of ideological convictions and religious principles which Swift retained throughout his life and writing career. The most curious feature of this controversy was the way Swift's conservatism was mistaken for the very thing it sought to expose – extremism. The 'Apology' attacks readers so literal-minded that they confuse the tactical style with actual intention, miss the irony of the text, and declare its author as blasphemous:

> Why should any Clergyman of our Church be angry to see the
> Follies of Fanaticism and Superstition exposed, tho' in the most
> ridiculous Manner? since that is perhaps the most probable way
> to cure them, or at least to hinder them from farther spreading.
> Besides, tho' it was not intended for their Perusal; it raillies
> nothing but what they preach against. It contains nothing to
> provoke them by the least Scurillity upon their Persons or their
> Functions. It celebrates the Church of England as the most
> perfect of all others in Discipline and Doctrine, it advances no
> opinion they reject, nor condemns any they receive.[34]

Many contemporary readers, especially influential clergymen,
were blind to the subtleties of the irony which Swift deployed in
attacking religious fanaticism. To an outraged Swift, this showed
deplorable literary taste. These dull critics had failed to see the
point and necessity of a radical form for a conventional theme. The
combination of conventional religion and subversive artistic form
created a dangerous and difficult chemistry for many observers
who mistook parody for endorsement. If the author of the *Tale* had
come so close to the spirit of fanaticism, they argued, perhaps he
had been infected with it. In this tension between form and
purpose lay Swift's clerical and literary dilemma. Thinking to serve
his Church through literary originality, he had risked being seen as
one of those lunatics he actually wanted to exclude from the State.
It is not difficult to appreciate his anger with this muddled
religious response: if the madness of his literary creation was
attributed to his personality, it would hardly provide a worthy
reference for the country vicar from Ireland who wanted to settle in
England.

The 'Apology', and the accompanying satires against religious,
political and literary extremism, suggest a deep conflict between
the clerical and artistic sides to Swift's personality, between the
responsible and the playful. He acknowledges that the satires were
the product of earlier exuberance, 'finished above thirteen Years
since ... The Author was then young, his Invention at the Height,
and his Reading fresh in his Head'. The present indignation and
fuss, he suggests, has been brought about by people with little
imagination and no sense of fun. He declares that such lively and
sophisticated writing was written only for 'Men of Wit and Tast',

who require no solemn explication of the author's message in an admittedly difficult text. Criticism, says the author, is the principal enemy of humour.

As a parody of 'modern' writing, *A Tale Of A Tub* is intended to mock the vacuity and superficiality of contemporary English letters. By adopting the mask of a Grub Street hack trying to tell a story while constantly digressing, a story preceded and concluded by numerous literary formalities, Swift hoped to show the superiority of a classical literature which the hack despises. The allegorical heart of the *Tale*, based on a parable of religious schism and corruption, tends to be overwhelmed by the play on literary conventions and formal arrangements. Whatever Swift's intentions, the *Tale* is more memorable for its literary than its religious satire.

Only a classicist in touch with contemporary writing could achieve such command over a satire which displays abundant knowledge while exposing a total lack of discrimination. Himself a great formalist, Swift enjoys mocking the vanity which lies behind the contemporary vogue for texts consisting largely of ceremonial parts, for want of any genuine or original literary talent:

> Such is exactly the Fate, at this Time, of *Prefaces, Epistles, Advertissments, Introductions, Prolegomena's, Apparatus's, To the Reader's*. This Expedient was admirable at first: Our Great *Dryden* has long carried it as far as it would go, and with incredible Success. He has often said to me in Confidence, that the World would never have suspected him to be so great a Poet, if he had not assured them so frequently in his Prefaces, that it was impossible they could either doubt or forget it.[35]

This is one of many comic blunders by the nameless defender of modern letters. The hack is familiar with the great names of world literature, but defends the contemporary practice of selective abstraction, using short-cuts to arrive at the appearance of knowledge and learning: this is the advice of a shameless plagiarist who turns ignorance into a convenience, superficiality into a virtue. Swift's confidence and wit in representing this modern type comes from an early gift for literary ventriloquism. The risk he took, of course, was of being confused with the dummy. He must create a character with a voice of its own, a style which must not be undermined by the dullness which it hopes to expose, and a

mentality which is consistently blind to the contradictions of its
sweeping pronouncements. The art of mimicry would always
remain one of Swift's greatest talents.

Another original and enduring feature of Swift's style in these
early satires is the ironic use of homely aphorism, often extending
into an elaborate conceit. At the conclusion of the *Tale*, the hack
ponders the problem of difficult and mysterious books:

> I have one Word to say upon the Subject of *Profound Writers*,
> who are grown very numerous of late; And know very well, the
> judicious World is resolved to list me in that Number. I conceive
> therefor, as to the Business of being *Profound*, that it is with
> *Writers*, as with *Wells*; A Person with good Eyes may see to the
> Bottom of the deepest, provided any *Water* be there; and, that
> often, when there is nothing in the World at the Bottom, besides
> *Dryness and Dirt*, tho' it be but a Yard and half under Ground, it
> shall pass, however, for wondrous *Deep*, upon no wiser a Reason
> than because it is wondrous *Dark*.[36]

The speaker's irritation with profundity comes from envy of work
more substantial than his own. But the conceit serves a dual
purpose. It also allows Swift to have a dig at another 'modern'
wonder – literary criticism – for him a pseudo-science more like the
superstition of religious fanaticism than reasoned observations by
men of taste. The critical pursuit of mysteries in literature was as
foolish as the speculation on religious mysteries was dangerous.
By 1710, Swift could speak with experience of the folly of criticism,
since several commentaries, keys and guides to earlier editions of
the *Tale* had appeared or were being prepared.[37] It is not unac-
teristic of Swift that he contributed some serious, some ironic,
critical commentary of his own to Tooke's edition. However, most
of Swift's own notes provide sources for the wealth of classical
allusion and quotation in the *Tale*.

The accompanying satires, *The Battle Of The Books* and *The
Mechanical Operation Of The Spirit*, reinforce the earlier image of a
youthful writer with classical values satirising contemporary
thought through radical forms of parody. These two shorter satires
deal, respectively, with the brash and vulgar character of modern
writing and religious dissent. Religion and literature were the
combined targets of parody in the alternating structure of the *Tale*:
now each is dealt with separately in order to finish them off. Why,

however, does Swift make this identification between religious and literary madness? What does a 'modern' writer have in common with a religious crank? Swift asserts that the hack and the zealot share the same contempt for traditional values which he associates with a more civilised social order in culture and religion. The religious enthusiast is usually a literary philistine, while the modern writer, even if religiously sane, contributes to the general disrespect for the past. To use Swift's own favourite image of contempt, the poetaster and the puritan are full of noxious wind.

This youthful defence of tradition gives a unique tension to the satires. Why should Swift be so committed to tradition at such a relatively early stage in his writing career? I think the answer to this is both social and personal. Most shaping influences on him were deeply conservative. Irish Anglicanism, precisely because it was threatened by Dissent, especially in the north, had to be ultra-conservative. Numerically as well as politically, it could not entertain toleration. Service to William Temple was, however, the overwhelming influence on Swift's literary taste, though not on his inventiveness.[38] Although the *Tale* and the *Battle* were written in a style utterly remote from that of Swift's patron and master, they are a paradoxical tribute to Temple's idea of culture. Being young and conservative is not necessarily a contradiction or a literary posture. Swift genuinely identified with most forms of religious and literary orthodoxy. Only a superficial reading of his style of defence would suggest otherwise.

The Battle Of The Books is the least ambiguous defence of classical culture amongst these early satires. Written during the composition of the *Tale*, it was intended as a polemical contribution to a literary debate in which Temple had been criticised for insufficient appreciation of modern writing and for always championing the unsurpassable achievements of Greek and Roman culture. Written in the form of a mock-epic confrontation between ancient and modern books in St James' Library, it is an elaborate drama of irreconcilable tastes. Marshalling the two armies like a military puppeteer, Swift characterises the Ancients as virtuous, brave and dignified, while the moderns are ruthless, cowardly and confused. Temple appears repeatedly in this allegorical drama as 'General of the Allies to the Ancients'. The outcome of the battle, of course, is never in doubt, and the interest lies more in Swift's elaborate allusiveness than in the narrative.

The modern assault on Parnassus, like that by Dissent on the

Established Church, is a dangerous revolution inspired by pride and envy. Its leaders, William Wotton and Richard Bentley, who had originally criticised Temple's uncompromising classicism, are portrayed as 'two Mungrel-Curs' without honour or principle. The Ancients, headed by Homer and Virgil, are god-like figures who thrash their enemies through superior wisdom and tact. The real allegorical villain of this battle is 'a malignant Deity call'd Criticism', portrayed as the destructive inspiration behind the conflict:

> At her right Hand sat *Ignorance*, her Father and Husband, blind with Age; at her left, *Pride*, her Mother, dressing her up in the Scraps of Paper herself had torn. There was *Opinion*, her sister, light of Foot, hoodwinkt, and headstrong, yet giddy and perpetually turning. About her played her Children, *Noise* and *Impudence*, *Dullness* and *Vanity*, *Positiveness*, *Pedantry* and *Ill-Manners*. The Goddess herself had Claws like a Cat: Her Head, and Ears, and Voice, resembled those of an *Ass*, Her Teeth fallen out before; her Eyes turned inward, as if she lookt only upon herself.[39]

This is a powerful, because sensational, image executed with patient relish for its hated subject. In keeping with Swift's defence of his cultural master, this new pseudo-science of literary criticism is typified as a rowdy upstart without breeding, a cross between a child and an animal. Swift is unbeatable at character-assassination, especially when he uses the language of the grotesque.

Some literary criticism, like most religious enthusiasm, was a destructive form of speculation which always provoked Swift's spleen. A convincing satire on these issues, like any effective polemic, must sound uncompromising. The energy and conviction behind the *Battle* comes largely from Swift's loyalty to his patron, a victim of unreasonable criticism. Equally, Swift could sound quite paranoid about opinions which simply conflicted with his own. He was not as anti-modern as this satire suggests, and we should always be careful to listen out for distinctions between the author and the persona.

The third and final satirical piece of the anonymous 1704 volume was *The Mechanical Operations Of The Spirit*. In style and content it is wholly consistent with the *Tale*, so much so that the 'Apology' of 1710 expresses surprise that it appears as a separate satire, whereas it was originally intended to lie within the *Tale*'s open and flexible structure. Blaming publishers and editors for misunderstanding his plans is a constant complaint with Swift; but in this context it is difficult to see whether he is being serious or ironic. In any event, *The Mechanical Operation* is a self-sufficient piece which parodies the much-abused literary convention of the formal epistle in order to satirise the spiritual pretensions of religious fanatics. Using a familiar mock-reasonableness, its author concludes that spiritual enthusiasm is the effect of sexual disorder.[40] Puritans, under this ironic scrutiny, are revealed as perverts.

The moral of this tailpiece expresses a view on the actual relation between the earthly and the heavenly, the sexual and the spiritual, which confirms Swift's essentially sceptical personality. Using the religious enthusiast as his model, Swift makes the following generalisation about all such apparent saintliness:

> ... however Spiritual Intrigues begin, they generally conclude like all others; they may branch upwards towards Heaven, but the Root is in the Earth. Too intense a Contemplation is not the Business of Flesh and Blood; it must by the necessary Course of Things, in a little Time, let go its Hold, and fall into *Matter*. Lovers, for the sake of Celestial Converse, are but another sort of *Platonicks*, who pretend to see Stars and Heaven in Ladies Eyes, and to look or think no lower; but the same *Pit* is provided for both; and they seem a perfect Moral to the Story of that Philosopher, who, while his Thoughts and Eyes were fixed upon *Constellations*, found himself seduced by his *lower Parts* into a *Ditch*.[41]

Passages like this seem to combine a familiar stylistic paradox found in Swiftian satire – a crude, schoolboy-glee in witnessing animal nature assert its primacy against all intellectual pretension, but expressed through a mature, sophisticated rhetoric. Swift's religious views are simple enough and certainly based on a no-nonsense theology which abhors the abuse of reason in idle pursuit of explanations for inexplicable authority. In literary terms, however, it is not so simple. Swift's profound anti-intellectualism, or rather his fear and distrust of the social and political consequences of revolutionary and innovative thinking, are usually expressed in a parasitic form which thrives off the very thing it wishes to exorcise. It is extremely rare to hear Swift express his real views in a serious manner. Without Dissent or pedantry, it is hard to imagine Swift as a writer.

A more concrete measure of Swift's literary taste during the composition of these satires is his personal reading.[42] Most of his books were classical works such as Virgil, Horace and Homer. But he also read, not surprisingly, a great deal of modern and contemporary English and French writing, especially travel literature. Rabelais seems to have been his favourite light reading. Cervantes and Marvell figure prominently in his annotated books. As Temple's secretary, Swift would also have supervised the extensive library at Moor Park. Despite the single-mindedness of the early satires, with their unyielding attack on modern pedantry and 'invention', (always a derogatory term for Swift), the personal reading shows great variety and even greater tolerance. This suggests that the orthodoxy of the satires is partly tactical, yet largely the result of conviction and preference. At the risk of stating the obvious – only someone very familiar with contemporary writing could subject its worst features to such effective abuse.

A Tale Of A Tub is Swift's first major literary achievement. Energetic, playful and learned, it has been described as a work 'more concerned with literature than anything else he ever wrote'.[43] It is, paradoxically, one of the most 'modern' of Swift's writings, with its deliberate and witty self-consciousness, its parodic skill, and its satirical manipulation of the literary and religious conventions of the late seventeenth century. Before *Gulliver's Travels*, it was also his most successful and popular work, going through ten editions in his lifetime, three of these in Dublin. It was quickly and repeatedly translated in Europe: before the end of the eighteenth century, five French translations appeared, four German and one Dutch.[44]

Swift's original mask of anonymity, and his defence of the *Tale* as the views of a moderate churchman, were soon lost and misunderstood. His desire to exercise caution in the interests of ambition was defeated by ensuing circumstances beyond his control. The spirit of the *Tale* would, in a few years after publication of the fifth edition, take revenge on its conservative but eccentric author, and determine the pattern of his clerical and literary career.

2

'Pox on the Dissenters and Independents!'

As secretary to a Lord Justice at the centre of the Irish administration, Swift began a more public life than in Moor Park with the retired Temple. Following Berkeley's movements between Dublin and London, he came into contact with new, influential figures in the political administration and the literary scene. After his first partisan pamphlet, the *Discourse*, and the secretive publication of the *Tale*, Swift published relatively little in the first decade of the new century. As so often in his career, he wrote more than he cared to publish, and even when he considered it opportune to submit work to a printer, it was invariably anonymous or pseudonymous. He had only once signed his name to a publication, and that was as editor of Temple's writings.

Despite Swift's talent and ambition, he was a literary amateur whose primary duty lay with the Church. However, pleasure and responsibility could regularly find a shared interest, and even Swift's most playful productions never lost an opportunity to defend the Church. In these early years as vicar of Laracor and secretary to Berkeley, new controversies of State and Religion attracted his mental energies. The most important and obsessive of these controversies was whether the government in London would introduce legislation to repeal discriminatory laws against Dissenters in Ireland. Under the Sacramental Test, all non-conforming Protestants, especially Presbyterians, were debarred from civic, military and judicial posts unless and until they agreed, through occasional conformity, to recognise the supreme authority of the Established Church. Swift's characterisation of Dissent as a dangerous form of political and religious lunacy was already a dominant feature of the early satires. But literature could not compete with legislation. Proposals to tolerate Dissent became the subject for Swift's most paranoid writings, a challenge to his political and clerical integrity.

Deciding to write pamphlets against Toleration was not a simple choice for Swift. Always alert to absurdity, part of him felt that joining in the pamphlet-war was to adopt a form whose tone and content could too easily become the victim of convention. Agreeing with people was one thing, writing like them was another. Easily bored with solemn denunciation of non-conformity, Swift's artistic ego is often offended by literary conformity. In a letter from London to his friend in Dublin, Rev. William Tisdall, Swift describes pamphlets on this vexed issue as 'usually the vilest things in nature'. Part of this aloofness comes from his temporary hope and illusion that he belonged to England, and that Irish affairs were beneath him. His contempt for the form is explained, too literally, by his disgust for the subject: 'Pox on the Dissenters and Independents! I would as soon trouble my head to write against a louse or a flea.'[1] Dissenters may be a minor irritation, but they become magnified by Swift's fear and intolerance into the major fixation of his writing career. He would love to ignore them, but decides the risk of conventional attack is sometimes preferable to original silence.

The years 1704–7 are largely a biographical blank in Swift's career.[2] Only three letters survive from this period, two on Church business, the third to John Temple, a nephew of Sir William. In this letter we get a witty hint of Swift's ironic resignation to life at home – 'If I love Ireland better than I did, it is because we are nearer related, for I am deeply allyed to its Poverty.'[3] But this interregnum did have some personal and literary rewards. Spending much of his time around Dublin Castle with the new Lord Lieutenant, the Earl of Pembroke, Swift wrote several short pieces for fun and diversion, with no intention of immediate publication. These included *A Meditation On A Broomstick*, dated August 1704, a parody of scientific reflection written to amuse Lady Berkeley; *Thoughts on Various Subjects*, dated October 1706, a collection of aphorisms and maxims; and *A Tritical Essay Upon the Faculties of the Mind*, dated August 1707, written for a friend, Andrew Fountaine, usher to the Earl of Pembroke, in which Swift parodies a learned style base on endless cliché.

The aphoristic *Thoughts* are of special literary interest, if only because they seem to express Swift's views without the protective distraction of irony. Clearly influenced by La Rochefoucauld, they cover a wide range of subjects with opinionated wit and concise elegance. Beginning with the oft-quoted paradox, 'We have just Religion enough to make us *hate*, but not enough to make us *love* one another' (Swift would reject any suggestion of a double standard on this one), he makes several observations about literature and writers:

> If a Writer would know how to behave himself with relation to Posterity; let him consider in old Books, what he finds, that he is glad to know; and what Omissions he most laments.
> ...
> When a true Genius appears in the World, you may know him by this infallible Sign; that the Dunces are all in Confederacy against him.
> ...
> It is grown a Word of Course for Writers to say, this *critical Age* as Divines say, this sinful Age.[4]

We remember Swift's treatment of literary and religious critics in the *Tale*: this conjunction between criticism and sin is a consistent element of a puritanical aesthetic. Since we know that Swift was still aiming for some preferment in England through new political contracts, the remarks on ambition are of special biographical interest:

> It is a miserable Thing to live in Suspence; it is the Life of a Spider.
> ...
> Ambition often puts Men upon doing the meanest Offices; so climbing is performed in the same Posture with Creeping.[5]

Self-criticism is a guide to personal consistency. An inveterate hater of useless speculation, Swift preferred opinions formulated to reflect upon and encourage moral behaviour in civil society. The systematic form of these *Thoughts*, like the regularly itemised accounts of his housekeeping, points to a literary species of rectitude not often acknowledged in Swift.

These three diversionary pieces were not published together until 1711,[6] but were obviously circulated amongst Swift's friends for entertainment. Always a tactician, he kept his own copies in case sportive writings like these might, in circumstances more congenial to his ambition, find their place alongside weightier matter. One more substantial prose work written during this comparatively quiet period deserves note. This is Swift's first pamphlet on Irish affairs, *The Story of the Injured Lady*, written around May 1707, near the end of a three-year stay in Ireland.

The *Story* was occasioned by the proposed Act of Union between England and Scotland, announced in January of that year and settled in May. The theme of this allegorical piece is suggested by its sub-title, 'A True Picture of Scotch Perfidy, Irish Poverty, and English Partiality'. Swift, like many others in Ireland, was outraged that Irish Protestants loyal to the Crown should see England granting Scotland constitutional and legal favours denied to Ireland. In this story of betrayal, the woman/Ireland complains to a friend that her lover/England has abandoned her in favour of a shrewish mistress/Scotland. This is not a medium for sophisticated or reasonable analysis, but an opportunity to personalise and simplify history through caricature. The image of Scotland is polemical and graphic:

> As to her Person she is tall and lean, and very ill-shaped; she hath bad Features, and a worse Complexion; she hath a stinking Breath, and twenty ill Smells about her besides; which are yet more insufferable by her natural Sluttishness; for she is always lousy, and never without the Itch.[7]

The loathing behind this portrait threatens to break out into the scatological style most often associated with Swift's verse, but is here held in check by the more positive element in the allegory. Yet Swift cannot resist breaking through this fiction in order to clinch his case against this offensive Union: 'To conclude her Character; she is of a different Religion, being a Presbyterian of the most rank and virulent Kind.' That last defining clause is deceptive since for Swift the type permitted no variation: the Dissenter is essentially and always a witch. In a brief *Answer to the Injured Lady*, a friend consoles her by recommending practical proposals which will guarantee autonomy, self-respect and prosperity. Decoded from their chivalric medium, these proposals are the basis of Swift's programme of reforms for an Irish economy free from English control and interference. That programme, first outlined in the *Story*, was simple and aggressive, demanding a boycott of all unnecessary imports, a drive towards greater self-reliance, and the right to trade without legislative obstruction from London.

The *Story* reminds us that Swift could still feel strongly defensive about his birthplace, notwithstanding his Anglophile manner. It is his first piece of patriotic writing, in which English colonialism is criticised. Much later on in his career, as Dean and Drapier, he would use identical arguments and proposals, but free from the restrictive and artificial form of romantic allegory. The *Story* reveals an important, because hidden, side to Swift's writing at this time. Trying for an English post, making repeated approaches to English Whig politicians, he clearly decided that Irish patriotism of this kind would hardly endear him to London. He put it aside and concentrated on other writings more in tune with contemporary sympathies. It was never published in his lifetime, eventually appearing in 1746, in both London and Dublin.

This relative lull in literary activity was followed by a stay in England which brought Swift, for the first time, into personal contact with London's literary élite. On 29 November 1707, the day before his fortieth birthday, he left Ireland as part of the Lord Lieutenant's entourage. His principal business was to act as unofficial representative for the Church of Ireland in its efforts to secure remission of the First Fruits, a tax levied on the Church by the government. Swift must have felt that he was following the diplomatic tradition of Temple, dealing with government ministers and the Court over the nation's affairs. To his vexation, the clerical enterprise dragged on for months, leaving him sitting outside many courtly offices, disappointed and weary, lacking any real power to grace his imagined role of clerical ambassador.

While enduring 'the Life of a Spider', Swift was introduced to two of London's most popular and influential writers, Joseph Addison and Richard Steele. Addison was a favourite of the Whigs, for whom he wrote many pamphlets defending the war against France. He was also quite an influential political figure, as Under-Secretary of State to Lord Sutherland. Steele, a Dubliner by birth, was editor of the *London Gazette*, the government newspaper. While this was a literary friendship in which Addison and Steele were delighted to meet the author of the *Discourse* and the *Tale*, it was also a connection with important career possibilities. As Ehrenpreis puts it, these London writers belonged to a set of 'literary sinecure-hunters', which included Matthew Prior and Swift's old college acquaintance, William Congreve.[8] He could see that these writers of the 'Kit-Kat' club, sponsored by the Whig government, all had enviable political protection and literary security. Aristocratic patronage of writers was here replaced by political investment in people with literary talent whom the government could employ and reward. Since Swift considered himself, especially in affairs of State, as an 'old-fashioned Whig', he did not foresee any difficulty in mixing politics and literature. For the moment, writing and partisanship seemed naturally compatible.

Swift's relaxation from Church business began with a playful masquerade. In January 1708, he published the first of a series of pamphlets and broadsides using one of his most famous masks. Entitled *Predictions for the Year 1708*, and using the pseudonym Isaac Bickerstaff, it is a mocking parody of the astrological almanac. Posing as the genuine article, Bickerstaff deplores astrology's low reputation, and promises a 'rational Defence of this Art'. Conceding that the practice suffers many predictable abuses, he promises 'to proceed in a new Way'. He first predicts the death of 'Partridge the Almanack-Maker':

> I have consulted the Star of his Nativity by my own Rules; and find he will infallibly die upon 29th of March next, about eleven at Night, of a raging Fever: Therefore I advise him to consider of it, and settle his Affairs in Time.[9]

This casual opening prediction of the death of a fellow-astrologer 'is but a Trifle', and yet the occasion for the entire hoax. Partridge was a well-known almanac-maker in London, who regularly lampooned the Church of England in lines like the following:

> High-Church! the common Curse, the Nation's Shame.
> Tis only Pop'ry by another Name.[10]

By voicing such anti-clerical abuse, and simultaneously dealing in scientific quackery, Partridge was the perfect embodiment of everything Swift scorned. Having forecasted the trickster's death, Bickerstaff then predicts a host of political crises in Europe, most of them afflicting England's enemies. A blatantly partisan convention of the form, this flattery posing as science was one of the most absurd features of such commercial speculation. The *Predictions* are a perfect literary prank, but their inspiration is quite serious. On occasions like this, Swift is like a literary sleuth as far as free-thinkers are concerned.

The pamphlet was an instant, yet pseudonymous, success. Many pirated editions appeared in London within a few days, and it seemed that all literary tastes enjoyed the pasquinade on Partridge. In February, to encourage confusion, Swift wrote *An Answer to Bickerstaff*, 'By a Person of Quality', questioning the value of the *Predictions* and generally deploring their appeal to Grub Street taste for the sensational. Recalling Bickerstaff's promise of more predictions, this gentleman-critic sarcastically remarks that it will probably contain such gems as *The General History of Ears*. This was a sneaky allusion to one of Swift's own parodic titles, mentioned in the preface to *A Tale Of A Tub*, already in its fourth edition. Preferring complete, if only temporary, disguise, he dropped the clue and withheld the *Answer*. But the sport with Partridge continued, and at the end of March appeared *An Account of the Death of Mr Partridge*, a morbidly playful celebration of the astrologer's painful death and Bickerstaff's wonderful foresight. Written by an 'independent' witness at Partridge's death-bed, the writer confirms that Bickerstaff had indeed been responsible for the poor man's decline into insanity and delirium. On a note of vengeful poetic justice, the observer concludes that, on his death-bed, Partridge '. . . declared himself a Nonconformist, and had a fanatick Preacher to be his spiritual Guide'. This allegorical image of Lunacy assisted by Fanaticism is the moral epitaph to Swift's imaginative execution of one of London's best-known quacks.

This game of impersonation and disguise, in which the line between fact and fiction had become comically blurred, must have delighted Swift's sense of vicarious power. The literary sport reached its climax a year after it began when, early in 1709, Partridge rose to the bait and denounced Bickerstaff as a fraud. Swift retaliated with *A Vindication of Isaac Bickerstaff*, in which he resolutely denied Partridge's claim to be alive. In his best manner of patient, scholarly refutation, he points to his own international standing as a serious astrologer, and claims that his 'Concern is not so much for my own Reputation, as that of the Republick of Letters'. Adopting the pose of a disinterested reasoner dedicated to impartial truth, he declares Partridge to be an 'uninformed Carcass', despite any assertion to the contrary. Reversing his own ironic strategy, he deplores the current taste for trivialising serious matters. He notes that '. . . it is the talent of our Age and Nation, to turn Things of the greatest Importance into Ridicule'. By taking seriously the ludicrous speculations of astrology, Swift effectively satirises both pedantry and superstition.

Several other well-known literary figures joined in, or were taken in. *Squire Bickerstaff Detected*, a mock-refutation by Partridge, was attributed by Addison to Congreve.[11] In this variation of the general confusion between the authentic and the parodic, the writer accuses Bickerstaff of being part of a Papish conspiracy aimed at 'a general Massacre of Learning'. Richard Steele, observing the progress of this comic deception, approached Swift about using the Bickerstaff persona and spirit for contributions to the *Tatler*, a new paper he was planning.[12] After it began, in April 1709, Steele acknowledged the inspirational figure of Bickerstaff for this new literary venture. The final, and most triumphant, deception came with Swift's *Famous Prediction of Merlin*, written in 1709, a clever imitation of a sixteenth-century prophecy telling of events to come in 1709! To enhance the forgery, Swift had it drawn up in Gothic black-letter to simulate an 'ancient' style, and wrote a scholarly series of annotations on many of the more cryptic details of the manuscript. The predictions, needless to say, were amazingly accurate.

Although he enjoyed the popular reign of Bickerstaff in literary London, Swift had serious clerical business to pursue, a duty which contrasted miserably with the sport of fiction. As part of his efforts to secure remission of the First Fruits from the government, he had eventually succeeded, after six months waiting, in talking directly to the Lord Treasurer. This humiliating interview, in which Swift was told that the government would consider the proposal if certain 'Acknowledgements' were made by the Irish Church, was relayed in full in a letter of June 1708 to Archbishop King in Dublin.[13] It was clear that the government wanted to trade remission of taxes for an agreement to grant Toleration to Dissenters in Ireland. To gall him further, Swift knew that these taxes had been lifted from the English clergy four years beforehand. 'English Partiality' was becoming familiar. Swift was also made to feel that, as a lowly vicar, he had overstepped the mark by assuming such diplomatic airs. He apologised to Archbishop King for such a 'lame and tedious' account, one which would only have intensified Swift's emotion with regard to Dissent.

During the summer of 1708, Swift started to write a series of tracts and pamphlets exposing the claims of non-conformists to legal toleration. This was in response to a growing lobby determined to repeal the Sacramental Test. Bickerstaff had been a literary sport: Toleration became a literary war. Swift began to assemble his various writings with his eye on a single volume which he hoped Steele would publish in 1709 as his *Miscellanies*.[14] He wrote to Ambrose Philips, a literary friend shared with Addison, 'I am every day writing my Speculations in my Chamber.'[15] He had abandoned an essay, *Remarks upon Tindall's Rights of the Christian Church*, which had attacked Tindall's case that the Anglican Church wanted to be, like Rome, a law unto itself. This piece had become bogged down in legalistic refutation, a form of counter-reasoning which suffered from those very defects of style which Swift deplored in others. His own reasonable manner sometimes slips too easily into self-parody: his most effective manner is polemical and passionate, not reasonable and restrained.

The first completed essay was *The Sentiments of a Church-of-England Man with Respect to Religion and Government*. Free from any ironic intent, it is a serious and impassioned statement of what he believes to be a reasonable and incontrovertible outlook: 'I have gone as far as I am able in qualifying my self to be such a Moderator: I believe, I am no Bigot in Religion; and I am sure, I am none in Government.'[16] It is always intriguing, even slightly shocking, for modern readers to see Swift's polemical tracts use terms like 'Moderation' to defend his own sectarianism while using the same terms to identify the mischievous language of his opponents. Swift is a man of moderate views: his enemies, all fanatics, pretend to be moderate. Give them an inch, and reason will be overwhelmed. If tracts like the *Sentiments* had aimed for some kind of liberal impartiality, then Swift would have seen them as worse than useless. The author points to his anonymity as concrete proof of his objectivity, before beginning his vendetta against those who dare question the soundness of his orthodoxy.

Many of the views expressed in the *Sentiments* echo those of the 1701 *Discourse*, especially the conventional Whig commitment to balance of power within the State, and the need to avoid all forms of tyranny. With the Sacramental Test currently an issue, he singles out Dissenters and their literary apologists as the most dangerous threat to constitutional stability. Always keen to display his historical knowledge, Swift selects examples from classical history and the Cromwellian period to prove the folly of compromise with trouble-makers. His paranoia about the infection of Dissent into the body politic leads him to recommend the closest supervision and censorship of subversive ideas:

> He thinks it a Scandal to Government, that such an unlimited
> Liberty should be allowed of publishing Books against those
> Doctrines in Religion, wherein all Christians have agreed; much
> more to connive at such Tracts as reject all Revelation, and, by
> their Consequence, often deny the very Being of a God.[17]

Strictures like these remind us that Swift is first a priest and only
then a writer. His unconditional loyalty is to the Church established by law. Writers, he believes, have a moral responsibility to
protect the authority and sustain the respect due to Church and
State: if they can be witty and entertaining in performance of that
duty, so much the better. Even the seemingly freakish *Tale* was
written to celebrate '. . . the Church of England as the most perfect
of all others in Discipline and Doctrine'. Yet because Swift is
always sensitive to the depressing effects of literary convention
upon style, he admits that 'a great deal hath been already said by
other Writers, upon this invidious and beaten Subject', thereby
trying to distinguish the force and originality of his own contribution. The manner of the *Sentiments*, reasonable despite the obvious
contradictions of its argument, does not allow Swift to exercise his
real potential.

His next essay, *An Argument against Abolishing Christianity*, is a
virtuoso performance of ironic impersonation wholly suited to
Swift's literary temperament. It is the outstanding piece of that
summer's work, as ingenious as the *Tale*, as crafty as Bickerstaff.
This mock-proposal is spoken by an anonymous gentleman, earnest and painstaking in manner, who respectfully opposes those
freethinkers who would abolish Christianity without first considering the consequences. Through a polite, even apologetic, style of
opposition to the outrageous project, the persona enjoys an
ambiguous position from which the compromiser and the fanatic
may be effectively pilloried. His argument is deceptively simple –
why abolish Christianity since it scarcely exists? The small residue
of superficial religion left in the land offers many advantages for
free-thinkers to exploit. This kind of formal religion will be very
easy to deal with, since it is mostly a matter of show. While entirely
sympathetic to the complaints of persecution heard from Dissenters, the persona tries to show them the folly of abolishing
Christianity and its rituals, since such a move would leave them

with nothing to complain about. The speaker is one of Swift's favourite dummies – the pragmatist who substitutes expediency for principle.

In one of the most caustic ironies of the *Argument*, he pleads for the preservation of nominal Christianity in the interests of contemporary writing:

> What wonderful Productions of Wit should we be deprived of, from those whose Genius, by continual Practice hath been wholly turned upon Raillery and Invectives against Religion; and would therefor never be able to shine or distinguish themselves upon any other Subject. We are daily complaining of the great Decline of Wit among us; and would we take away the greatest, perhaps the only Topick we have left? ... It is the wise Choice of the Subject that alone adorns and distinguishes the Writer. For had an hundred such Pens as these been employed on the Side of Religion, they would have immediately sunk into Silence and Oblivion.[18]

Once the premise of a degenerate age is established and accepted, the collusion between barbarism in religion and philistinism in learning seems logical and unremarkable. Writers who encourage controversy and speculation in religion should remember to stop short of destroying what nourishes them, otherwise their genius will be thwarted. Those authors Swift had in mind were all radical, Dissenting pamphleteers, including the Irish Presbyterian, Toland, and are systematically mentioned in the *Argument*'s case for self-interest to overcome understandable prejudice.

Although Swift always maintains that he is above any factional or party interest, he allows the speaker to defend the language of partisanship whenever Dissenters protest that such terms divide the Protestant family of churches. In this context, 'Presbyterian' and 'Church-of-England' stand for very real differences not to be simply forgotten by removing or changing the words:

> ... will any Man say, that if the Words *Whoring, Cheating, Lying, Stealing*, were, by Act of Parliament, ejected out of the *English* Tongue and Dictionaries; we should all awake next Morning chaste and temperate, honest and just, and Lovers of Truth. Is this a fair Consequence? ... Are Party and Faction rooted in Mens Hearts no deeper than Phrases borrowed from Religion; or founded upon no firmer Principles?[19]

Religion, he agrees, is merely 'nominal': but political differences are inescapably deep and beyond negotiation. The fool who thinks that words can be conveniently detached from the unpleasant realities they represent is a danger to civilisation. Words mean what they say: their inherited and fixed meanings must not be distorted by witless subversives. In other words, the Sacramental Test may be removed, but that does not mean that Dissent will disappear with it.

The *Argument* is Swift's most teasing commentary upon Dissenters and those who find any sympathy for their cause. For the literal-minded on either side of the controversy, it was bound to be bewildering. Swift had made the same points without impersonation or irony but the voice sounded tired of such a plodding procedure. At the risk of confusing even those he supports, his style is always more energetic in a complete fiction. Answering nonsense with a straight face never suits him, even though he regularly adopts this moralistic approach. Such a schizophrenic pattern in Swift's writings is well described by Ehrenpreis as 'the partnership of a clown and a preacher'.[20] This is to posit a psychological account for such a dualistic or contradictory pattern, an account both perceptive and convincing: but political strategy and literary opportunism play a complementary and conscious role in the style and presentation of these texts.

At the end of 1708, Swift had drawn up a long list of 'Subjects for a Volume', which would eventually appear in his *Miscellanies*.[21] The list mentioned a 'Project for Reformation of Manners', which quickly became his *Project for the Advancement of Religion and the Reformation of Manners*, one of only two pieces published by Swift during these years. Although the plan was to assemble enough material for a substantial volume in which a variety of forms and styles could be displayed to his advantage and credit, Swift decided to publish the *Project* independently. Written by 'A person of Quality', and dedicated to the Countess of Berkeley, it is one of Swift's most moralistic proposals for social reform 'in this projecting Age', and is entirely serious in its puritanical ambition. Based on a medieval view of social hierarchy, it proposes that the monarchy and the Court extirpate social vice by setting a supreme example, and that political promotion be granted only to those whose integrity has been assessed by paid inquisitors. It was such a conventional outburst against degeneracy that many mistook it for a parody.

The arts, especially the theatre, are not exempt from this witch-hunt. The proposer expresses outrage that most plays showing in London seem to make deceit a laughing matter, and often leave virtue unrewarded:

These and many more Corruptions of the Theatre, peculiar to our Age and Nation, need continue no longer than while the Court is content to connive at, or neglect them. Surely a Pension would not be ill employed on some Man of Wit, Learning, and Virtue, who might have Power to strike out every offensive, or unbecoming Passage from Plays already written, as well as those that may be offered to the Stage for the future. By which, and other wise Regulations, the theatre might become a very innocent and useful Diversion, instead of being a Scandal and Reproach of our Religion and Country.[22]

Sentiments like these should check any impulse to idealise Swift as a writer who would defend the republic of letters against any attack. His venomous intolerance in such a transparent essay as this shows a personality not too far removed from the obsessive types he usually ridicules. In its refinements for moral supervision it can only be matched by the ironic sophistication of *A Modest Proposal*, written twenty years later.

This humourless tirade against the theatre began publicly in 1698, with Collier's *A Short View of the Immorality and Profaneness of the English Stage*. Jeremy Collier, like Swift after him, was a fervent Tory Anglican in questions of public morality. Swift had such a literary sense of humour, it is perhaps not so surprising that he disliked the exhibitionism of theatrical humour. There is, however, no evidence that Swift was a theatre-goer: like many puritan critics, he probably felt attendance was irrelevant to righteous judgement. Judging from the text of the *Project*, he must have had late Restoration drama in mind, the work of George Farquhar and William Congreve, both Irishmen like himself. Farquhar's comedies, *The Recruiting Officer* and *The Beaux Stratagem*, both appeared on the London stage while Swift was drafting materials for his *Miscellanies*. He also planned to attack the increasing vogue for operas in London, writing to tell a friend, 'I design to set up a Party among the Wits to run them down.'[23] He was most probably the author of an article in an early *Tatler* which ridiculed Italian opera, comparing it to the cries of street-vendors, 'an Accent and Tone neither natural to Man or Beast'.[24]

Apart from literature, Swift had little interest in the arts. Writing, as Ehrenpreis points out, combined 'craftsmanship and morality' for Swift.[25] The vicar of Laracor trusted the written word above all other forms of imaginative and sensuous appeal. His scandalised reaction to the licentiousness of theatre places him firmly, and paradoxically, in the tradition of those puritans who, in his grandfather's time, had closed down the theatre, and who are characterised in his *Tale* as literary philistines.

Swift instructed Benjamin Tooke to publish the *Project* immediately. The Earl of Berkeley wrote to Swift (presumably his wife having shown him a copy), urging him to send it to the Queen.[26] A fulsome review by Steele quickly appeared in the *Tatler*. Swift's missionary sense must have genuinely put aside political ambition, at least temporarily, since writings like this were implicitly anti-Whig, and could scarcely endear him to the government. Soon, however, that anxiety was made redundant by a dramatic change of government.

Along with his *Project*, the only other tract which Swift decided to publish immediately after composition was *A Letter from a Member of the House of Commons in Ireland to a Member of the House of Commons in England, Concerning the Sacramental Test*. This semifictional letter was provoked by the Whig appointment of Dr Lambert, in November 1708, as chaplain to Ireland's new Lord Lieutenant, Thomas Wharton. Not only had Swift wanted the post, but Lambert immediately made it clear that he would use his position to encourage the repeal of the Test against Irish Dissenters.[27] Even though Swift usually saw himself as a Whig in affairs of State, he was always suspicious of their religious policy, especially their willingness to accommodate non-conformists in the interests of Protestant unity. What rankled him was the way Ireland was being used by the Whigs as a laboratory for such legislative change, in defiance of the expressed views of the Irish Houses.

The *Letter* is an energetic rebuke by a fictional, but representative, Irish MP, who reminds his English brother of a few home truths about Anglo–Irish relations. Much of its stylistic energy comes from Swift's anger at English interference in 'a Matter purely national'. He is particularly annoyed by English pamphleteers on this issue, whose writings are found in all of London's coffee-houses. The greatest offender is someone called Daniel Defoe, 'so grave, sentencious, dogmatised a Rogue, that there is no enduring him'. (Swift could not remember his name when the *Letter* was first printed, but recalled it for the 1711 volume.) Observations upon Ireland by Englishmen always touched a raw nerve in Swift, especially when their views were more liberal than his own. The tone of this *Letter* is often crudely sarcastic, sometimes witty:

> I do not frequently quote Poets, especially *English*, but I remember there is some of Mr *Cowley's* Love Verses, a Strain that I thought extraordinary at Fifteen, and have often since imagined it to be spoken by *Ireland*.
>
> > *Forbid it Heaven my Life should be Weigh'd*
> > *With her least Conveniency.*
>
> In short, whatever Advantage you propose to your selves by repealing the *Sacramental Test*, speak it out plainly, it is the best Argument you can use, for we value your Interest much more than our own. If your little Finger be sore, and you think a Poultice made of our *Vitals* will give it any Ease, speak the Word, and it shall be done.[28]

The *Letter* is about power not logic. It dismisses any proposed compromise with Dissenters because they are so uncompromising, and contemptuously illustrates the condition of the Catholic majority, the so-called 'enemy' of all good Protestants:

> ... we look upon them to be altogether as inconsiderable as the Women and Children. Their Lands are almost entirely taken away from them, and they are rendered uncapable of purchasing any more ... the common People without Leaders, without Discipline, or Natural Courage, being little better than *Hewers of Wood, and Drawers of Water*, are out of all Capacity of doing any Mischief, if they were ever so well inclined.[29]

A new depth in cold arrogance is reached towards the end of the *Letter*, when the speaker asserts that the Irish Houses will never submit to a change in the law proposed by England because, as the speaker puts it, '... We are the Majority, and We are in Possession'.

A triumphant dogmatism correct in law, but wishful thinking in practice. The *Letter* is one of many examples in Swift's writing which prompts difficult problems of aesthetic judgement. By any civilised standard, the mentality behind it is shamelessly thuggish: yet the style, by Swift's own rhetorical standard, is superb polemic.

The *Letter* was published anonymously in January 1709, and reprinted in Dublin the following autumn. This pamphlet was the most openly anti-Whig of anything he had written: since his literary friends were close to the government, anonymity hardly seemed worth the care. Writing to one of his best Irish friends, Charles Ford, a Meath landowner, Swift smiles at his own situation: '... I am not grown great, nor like to do so very soon.'[30] He had looked forward to settling in Vienna for a while, where Lord Berkeley was to take up a diplomatic post, but the plan fell through.[31] In another letter, to Robert Hunter, a former literary acquaintance from London and Governor of Virginia, Swift confessed his frustration and offers himself boldly for a post in the colony:

> I shall go for Ireland some Time in Summer, being not able to make my Friends in the Ministry consider my Merits, or their Promises, enough to keep me here; so that all my Hopes now terminate in my Bishoprick of Virginia.[32]

Swift's former friends in the Whig Party, Somers and Sutherland, were now in deep political crisis. The Tories, led by Robert Harley, were openly favoured by Queen Anne, and no political office seemed secure during the summer of 1709. Swift, seeing little prospect of promotion in such an unstable climate, started to head home to Laracor.

After nineteen months in England, Swift's mission for the Church had ended as an embarrassing flop. Yet he had written quite a variety of prose and verse between these fruitless visits to the Court. He had made good friends with Addison and Steele, and enjoyed his comic role as Bickerstaff and London's enthusiastic response. Through his stay the issue of toleration for Dissent had been his overriding literary obsession, expressed in alternating ironic and moralistic forms. He also began to see himself as more than an occasional writer: he was a cultured clergyman, sensitive to all contemporary issues, who could offer the public a range of serious and entertaining works. His efforts during these years suggest a writer who sees himself as the conscience of civil society, a literary watchdog ready to attack anyone who intrudes on his ideal of the uniform State.

During these years of zealous invective against Dissent, Swift had not neglected the art of verse. Although he wrote few poems, they show a relaxed, confident humour very rarely heard in the pamphlets. After the solemn Odes of his early years, the poetic style underwent a radical change in favour of hudibrastic verse, whose rhyming couplets Samuel Butler had first used, coincidentally, to ridicule Puritanism. Swift's subjects include witty variations on classical stories such as 'Baucis and Philemon', sympathetic character-sketches from domestic life, as with the popular 'Petition of Frances Harris', and, naturally, satirical broadsides against Partridge. One of the most evocative poems from this period is the famous 'Description of the Morning', in which London's awakening underworld is treated with a novel blend of pastoral affection and urban familiarity:

> Now hardly here and there a Hackney-Coach
> Appearing, show'd the Ruddy Morns Approach.
> Now Betty from her Master's Bed had flown,
> And softly stole to discompose her own.
> . . .
> The Turnkey now his Flock returning sees,
> Duly let out a Nights to steal for Fees.
> The watchful Bailiffs take their silent Stands,
> And School-Boys lag with Satchels in their Hands.[33]

There is irony here, but of a subdued and indulgent variety far removed from the elaborately self-conscious humour of the prose satires or the bitter sarcasm of the tracts. In April 1709, Steele printed it in the *Tatler*, the first of several contributions from Swift, who was now on his way home via Leicester, where he would visit his mother for the last time.

3

A Pact with Power

Swift's character and status as a writer was to undergo extraordinary changes in the next few years. From having been a minor clergyman with remarkable but occasional literary talent, and still desperately hoping for an English post worthy of his ambition, he quickly became official propagandist for the new, Tory government, dining and socialising with the most powerful political circles in England. His four years with the Tories were extremely prolific, yet the style of this period seems quite a surprise after the masked humour of earlier work. Although he became a party-writer, he remained an amateur one, believing that such a principle guaranteed artistic integrity and proved personal independence. Long-term preferment, he felt, was worthier and more politic than short-term reward. For the first and last time in his writing career, he was to serve the interests of power.

In August 1710, Queen Anne began to dismiss the Whig ministers, and it was clear that a new Tory government was imminent. At the end of that month, an expectant Swift sailed from Ireland (on the same boat as a nervous Lord Lieutenant Wharton), with the intention of being in London to observe and, hopefully, exploit the dramatic political change. This time, Swift had a letter from the Irish bishops designating him as official spokesman for the First Fruits. After his humiliation with the Whigs over this issue, he felt that the Tories would not use the *quid pro quo* of Toleration for such a favour.

Two days after landing, he stopped overnight at Chester, en route for London. That evening, Swift began to write a unique series of letters which would continue for almost three years. Later editors, not Swift, called it the *Journal to Stella*.[1] Swift intended it as a private correspondence between himself and his two lady-friends back in Dublin, Esther Johnson and Rebecca Dingley, although most of it was written for his beloved Stella alone. Having no idea how long the clerical business would take, he began a journal in the form of a daily diary which he usually sent at fortnightly intervals, telling of news, progress, acquaintances, and always enquiring after his friends' society and health. The *Journal* is organised in typically methodical fashion: Swift wrote every day, numbered each letter, and kept a regular count of the replies to his own letters. Eventually, the *Journal* reached sixty-five letters.[2] Unfortunately, Swift later destroyed the other half of his correspondence.

While the *Journal* is undoubtedly a mine of intimate and public detail for the psychological and historical approaches to Swift, its special literary character is rarely discussed.[3] Nothing else ever written by him captures its playful, 'natural' style of spontaneous observation and expression. Not intended for public scrutiny,[4] it is entirely free from the comic displays of the satirical pieces. It gives the impression of great, even frantic, energy, racing from one thought to another without care for formal transition or warning. It is one of Swift's most 'live' writings, especially in the sense it gives of the physical effort and pleasure of writing as a substitute for companionship and intimacy.

The secrecy and playfulness of that friendship is marked by Swift's use of code-names for himself and the two women, and the reversion to an infantile 'baby-talk' with its own system of spelling. Swift is 'Presto' (a sobriquet given him by the Duchess of Somerset), the ladies are 'MD' ('my dears'). The regular and systematic exchange of letters is a comfort and a relaxation which gradually builds up a fiction of closeness:

> . . . nothing gives Presto any sort of dream of happiness but a letter now and then from his own dearest MD. I love the expectation of it, and when it does not come, I comfort myself, that I have it yet to be happy with. Yes faith, and when I write to MD, I am happy too; it is just as if methinks you were here and I prating to you, and telling you where I have been: Well, says you, Presto, come, where have you been today? come, let's hear now.[5]

Swift often adopts the tone and language of a fatherly lover chastising wayward girls. This manner is heard in the extraordinary epithets used to address the ladies. His favourite is 'sluttikins'; also included are 'saucy sluts', 'Gog and Magog', 'you couple of jades', 'unreasonable baggage' and 'sawci doxi'. There is a teasing sexual innuendo throughout the *Journal*, as when Swift informs them that 'good boys must write to naughty girls', or when he tells them that their letter, by a kind of sneaking synecdoche, lies beside him in a warm bed while he composes a reply.

When editing these letters after Swift's death, cousin Deane Swift removed much of their 'baby' language, probably because such distortions suggested an irrational side to the writer which he wished to deny. Some passages were, however, left untouched, and 'interpreted' rather apologetically. What remains gives us a fascinating image of Swift's gamesmanship with language:

> Do you know what? when I am writing in our language I make up my mouth just as if I was speaking it. I caught myself at it just now . . . Poor Stella, won't Dingley leave her a little day-light to write to Presto? Well, well, we'll have day-light shortly, spight of her teeth; and zoo must cly Lele and Hele and Hele aden. Must loo mimitate pdfr, pay? Iss, and so la shall. And so leles fol ee rettle. Dood mollow.[6]

In what Swift called 'our little language', certain letters such as 'l' and 'r' are usually exchanged. Certain syllables are represented by some rough phonetic version of a lisping child, so that the editor 'translated' the end of this piece as, 'And so there's for your letter. Good morrow.' The passage also includes another code name for Swift, 'pdfr', a contraction of 'poor dear foolish rogue', and pronounced 'Podefar'.

While many of Swift's early editors and commentators found these games distasteful signs of latent idiocy, they should come as no surprise to readers familiar with his sense of impish humour and his playful self-consciousness about language. Also, this is a form in which the writer relaxes, free from the daily pressure of official or commissioned writing. It is not so unusual or even untypical when we remember Swift's lifelong enjoyment of punning, word-play, and various forms of literary impersonation. His conscious separation of the serious and the playful is heard in one of these letters when he concludes an entry by saying, 'But let me alone, sirrahs: for Presto is going to be very busy: not Presto, but t'other I.'

That 'other', as the *Journal* shows, was constantly occupied by the business of renewing old contacts, making new ones, and determined to clinch the First Fruits in such a way as to impress both his Church and the rising Tories. Reading the *Journal* is quite a shocking experience, because of its rapid transitions between this public world, the personal gestures, and the novelty of the form itself. One minute Swift is playing word-games, the next he is reporting on the intricacies of political diplomacy. The tension of this style lies in its unexpectedness, its seeming indifference to discrimination:

> No, Mr Addison does not go to Ireland this year: he pretended he would; but he is gone to Bath with pastoral Phillips, for his eyes – So now I have run over your letter; and I think this shall go tomorrow, which will be just a fortnight from the last, and brings things to the old form again after your ramble to Wexford, and mine to Windsor. Are there not many literal faults in my letters? I never read them over, and I fancy there are. What do you do then? do you guess my meaning; or are you acquainted with my manner of mistaking? I lost my handkerchief in the Mall tonight with Lord Radnor: but I made him walk with me to find it, and find it I did not.[7]

After two years of writing his *Journal*, Swift began to enjoy the freedom and spontaneity of its style and form, joking that ''tis as naturall as Mother's milk, now I am got into it'. No matter how depressed, frustrated or sick, he sustained this unique literary bond until the last days of his absence. Although usually employed as a documentary aid, the *Journal*'s style and energy deserve greater literary attention. It shows us, for example, Swift's un-masked love for Stella, and his readiness to express it simply and directly. Nostalgia and tenderness often conclude the daily report: 'God Almighty bless and preserve dearest little MD ... Farewell, dearest MD, and love Presto, who loves MD infinitely above all earthly things and who will.'[8] Along with this affection for Stella, there is an understandable sense of wishing to live a simpler life, so that the rural vicarage of Laracor is pictured over and over again in the correspondence. The hectic reportage often exhausts itself in a desire to capture and convey the dynamic nature of cosmopolitan and courtly life which so fascinates Swift. Stella and Laracor provide a kind of moral and emotional centre to the combustible energy of the letters.

The *Journal* ensures that Swift's stay in London over the next three years is one of the best-documented periods of his career, giving us a daily account of his social life and his literary activity. From it we learn that, immediately after settling into his new lodgings in Bury Street, St James's, he renewed contact with Addison and Steele, the three of them dining out together regularly. Even though Swift was now looking to the Tories, and his two friends were still content with Whig patronage, shared literary interests kept the trio together. Steele was still editor of his periodical, the *Tatler*, which had already published the Bickerstaff pieces and 'Description of the Morning'. Swift's first literary exercise in this time in London was a short prose-piece for the *Tatler*, printed three weeks after his arrival, on 28 September, which revised the character of Bickerstaff in order to pronounce upon changing fashions in literary language.

This essay, number CCXXX in the periodical, takes the form of a complaint to the famous astrologer, who is now posing as guardian of the language, concerning abuses and corruptions of style. The anonymous informant lays the blame for this linguistic deterioration on a modern obsession with jargon and slang, used by aspiring writers to display an easy familiarity with all aspects of the contemporary scene. Political cant is the worst offender. He imitates a typical piece of 'trendy' journalism:

> Tom begins to gi'mself Airs, because he's going with the Plenipo's. – 'Tis said the French King will bamboozel us agen, which 'causes many Speculations. The Jacks, and others of that Kidney, are very uppish, and alert upon't, as you may see by their Phizz's.[9]

The writer is offended by such racy informality with so important a subject, dismissing its sensationalism as 'altogether of the Gothick Strain', and 'directly contrary to the Example of the Greeks and Romans'. He treats with contempt the suggestion that such writing shows a more logical relation between speech and spelling – 'A noble Standard for Language!' – and appeals to Bickerstaff to use his authority as censor to set up an annual Index Expurgatorius to cleanse and regulate the language of literature. In his humble opinion, the finest writing is that which follows the principle of 'Simplicity', which he describes as 'the best and truest Ornament of most Things in human life'.

The conservatism of this piece will come as no surprise, even though the idea of linguistic control may at first seem eccentric. The importance of this piece lies in the larger context of Swift's own political journalism and in his various, later projects for a national Academy to supervise and classify the process of linguistic change. His defence of classical taste against modern tastelessness can be quite misleading, if we associate 'classical' with some vague idea of 'lofty' prose packed with Greek and Roman allusions employed to dazzle and bewilder the general reader. He emphatically disliked a 'racy' style when dealing with serious matters like the constitution or international diplomacy. His idea of 'Simplicity' is, in fact, quite 'modern', if by that we mean a direct style suited to the occasion and aimed at an educated audience willing to learn. At this stage, Swift had yet to put such principles into practice. This preliminary essay went down well, and he wrote to Dublin, 'It is much liked here, and I think it is a pure one.'

Despite the tense political atmosphere, which would produce changes affecting patronage and loyalties amongst writers, Swift tried his best to maintain the literary friendship with Addison and Steele. A fortnight after his first *Tatler* contribution, he wrote, 'I am now writing my poetical *Description of a Shower in London*, and will send it to the *Tatler*.' This mock-georgic evocation of the metropolis appeared on 17 October, and was extremely popular. Although most of Swift's literary energy went into his prose writings, he could still show great accomplishment as a poet. This 'Description' is enriched by both his classical knowledge of Virgil and his familiarity with modern imitators, especially Dryden. Its easy, confident rhyming couplets present a detailed and observant picture of Nature overwhelming Civilisation, its rhythm alternating pastoral sublimity with urban bathos:

> Mean while the South rising with dabbled Wings,
> A Sable Cloud a-thwart the Welkin flings,
> That swill'd more Liquor than it could contain
> And like a Drunkard gives it up again.[10]

This relaxed movement between the two styles, forcing them into a new, humorous relation which produces an indulgent, mock-epic effect is the source of the poem's lively and original perspective. Swift does not miss a chance to make specific allusion to contemporary divisions swept aside in the general levelling brought about by the deluge: 'Triumphant Tories, and desponding Whigs, Forget their Fewds, and join to save their Wigs'. He concludes this witty apocalypse by parodying the technical innovations introduced by Dryden in this kind of epic verse, which mixed triple-rhymes and alexandrines with the more usual couplets and pentameter, an irregularity which offended the meticulous Swift:

Sweepings from Butchers Stalls, Dung, Guts, and Blood,
Drown'd Puppies, stinking Sprats, all drench'd in Mud,
Dead Cats and Turnip-Tops come tumbling down the Flood.[11]

Parody remained one of Swift's characteristic ways of asserting literary mastery and authority.

The evening of its publication, Swift wrote in his night-time letter, 'They say 'tis the best thing I ever writ, and I think so too.' Addison, Nicholas Rowe and Matthew Prior congratulated him warmly. Swift, feeling top of the class, wrote, '. . . they fell commending my *Shower* beyond any thing that has been written of the kind: there never was such a shower since Danaë's.' He mentioned it repeatedly in the *Journal*, wondering whether the ladies had seen it, and asking when it would be printed in Dublin. Eventually, at the end of November, he was glad to hear of their approval, though many Irish readers did not recognise some of the allusions to people and places in London. The Bishop of Clogher even confused this 'Description' with the one of the previous year, to which Swift retorted, 'I suppose he means *The Morning*; but it is not half so good.' The new poem obviously meant a great deal to Swift, possibly because writing poetry was not his recognised talent, and yet the poem was being applauded by London's best-known writers. Also, the poem was a display of pure literary skill and imagination, a piece which could not provoke political controversy or factional judgement. Finally, it showed him that, even though an outsider and a newcomer, he had given Londoners a picture of their city which reflected wordly confidence and urban familiarity, qualities he knew were indispensable in the circles he wished to cultivate.

Even though he was now an official representative for the Church of Ireland, he did not meet with immediate success over the First Fruits question. Most English politicians had, understandably, other priorities. In his second letter to Stella, the first from London, Swift wrote triumphantly, 'The Whigs were ravished to see me, and would lay hold on me as a twig while they are drowning, and the great men making me their clumsy apologies.' But, rather tactlessly, he went straight to Godolphin, the Whig Lord Treasurer who had been dismissed the previous month, and met with abrupt indifference. Never tolerating a snub, he wrote that evening, '. . . my Lord Treasurer received me with a great deal of coldness, which has enraged me so, I am almost vowing revenge.' Three weeks later, he confided, 'I have almost finished my lampoon, and will print it for revenge.' Literary reprisal appeared as 'The Virtues of Sid Hamet the Magician's Rod', a poetical satire on Godolphin's hypocritical character and abuse of office. The 'Rod', ostensibly the parliamentary symbol of that office, is exploited by Swift for purposes of sexual innuendo. The finished product, about ninety lines of dogged rhyme, is weighed down by excessive allusion to contemporary and classical figures. Personal malice often inspired forceful, passionate writing by Swift, but not this time.

However, Swift was delighted with his prank, and mentions it in the *Journal* nearly as often as the vastly superior 'Description'. A month after its appearance, he wrote to Stella:

> Have you heard of the verses about the *Rod of Sid Hamet*? Say nothing of them for your life. Hardly any body suspects me for them, only they think no-body but Prior or I could write them. But I doubt they have not reached you.[12]

Personal slander and character assassination, however distasteful, become distinctive features of Swift's literary output over the next few years. Obsessively cautious about protecting his own character, he thrived on mauling that of others.

He need not have worried, for the moment, about the ability of fallen Whigs like Godolphin to strike back. The Tories were in all the important ministerial posts: now they would control and dispense favour and preferment. Swift knew that they had their eye on him: 'The Tories dryly tell me, I may make my fortune, if I please; but I do not understand them, or rather, I do understand them.'[13] The afterthought shows clearly that Swift knew a bargain could be arranged. On 4 October, he was introduced to Robert Harley, the new Chancellor of the Exchequer, and was received, in his own words, 'with the greatest respect and kindness imaginable'. By mid-October, Harley had promised action on the First Fruits, and was calling the attentive vicar by his Christian name. The two men dined regularly at Harley's home, and Swift, obviously flattered and delighted by such intimacy, wrote home, 'I am to dine tomorrow at Mr Harley's; and if he continues as he has begun,

no man has been ever better treated by another.' But Harley saw
that granting the business request of the Irish vicar was a very
small price to pay for the literary services of a man whose
polemical talents were so promising.

Since so many writers like Steele and Addison had enjoyed the
patronage of the Whigs, Harley needed someone exempt from
such a close political affiliation, someone who could champion the
new government's case, especially its press campaign for a peace
in Europe to end the War of the Spanish Succession. More
specifically, the Tory Secretary of State, Henry St John, wanted a
writer to take over the government's new paper, the *Examiner*.[14]
Harley, now elevated to Earl of Oxford and Lord Treasurer, offered
Swift the job, which was promptly accepted.

Political patronage was the decisive factor in most literary
practices, affecting the prospects, livelihoods and even pensions of
journalists, dramatists, poets and printers. Steele had been dismissed from his post as editor of the *Gazette*, another government
mouthpiece, for having attacked Harley in the *Tatler*, and soon lost
another government sinecure in the Stamp Office. Swift was
extremely lucky that circumstance and need attracted the Tories to
him. Feeling betrayed and insulted by the Whigs, he could accept
the alternative patronage as a matter of principle and personal
pride.

He assumed the anonymous role of the *Examiner* in the first
week of November 1710, and wrote a weekly article until the first
week of June 1711, contributing thirty-three articles. As Tory
propagandist, his job was to emphasise the merits of party policy
and, equally important, to revile the Whigs. This task ended when
parliament rose for the summer recess. Within educated, influential political circles, he was now one of the most widely read
columnists in England. Using what Ehrenpreis calls 'the rhetoric of
impartiality', he adopted the manner of a disinterested but critical
observer, attached to no party, who was freely and genuinely
convinced of the natural superiority of Tory rule. This mask of
reasonable but spirited independence is crucial to the *Examiner*,
and Swift rarely displays a hint of partisan hysteria which could be
used to dismiss the articles as the work of a bigoted hack. The real,
as opposed to rhetorical, purpose of the job was to portray the
Whigs as war-mongers, unpatriotic and financially corrupt. The
fiction of magisterial independence made such a slanderous project all the more readable.

Swift's case against the Whigs, hammered home relentlessly and with pitiless energy, is that they represent a factional, subversive interest which is incompatible with the overwhelming support of the nation for the Established Church and the Constitution. His favourite tactic is to characterise all critics as conspirators, while representing the Tories as patriots above party. To heighten this emotional distinction, the Whigs are referred to as a 'monied interest', whose influence in banking and the Stock Exchange explains their support for a war which the rest of the nation opposes. The *Examiner* under Swift rewrites the politics of class by a drastic and moralistic simplification. The Tories, for example, many but not all of them from the landed gentry, represent the 'natural' spokesmen for traditional values of peace and prosperity. Swift establishes, or rather revives, an old-fashioned social hierarchy by such assertion: its appeal is to security, stability and conservatism. Of course, his role as propagandist was made easier by circumstances. To defend those who sought to end an expensive war required no ingenious argument; to attack those who insisted on its continuation gave Swift the moral high ground. Reason and a version of natural justice were on his side.

The rhetorical effectiveness of the *Examiner* comes from its confident balance between an authoritative and a homely style. It must always sound superior in knowledge, but never lose a tactful sense of expressing evident truths available to all. When he makes an assertion, Swift nearly always follows with a classical or popular analogy, as in the following passage where he uses a mythological conceit to illustrate the government's sense of responsibility after the chaos bequeathed by the Whigs:

> It makes me think of Neptune's Threat to the Winds: *Quos ego – sed motos praestat componere fluctus.* Thus, when the Sons of *Aeolus* had almost sunk the Ship with the Tempests they raised, it was necessary to smooth the Ocean, and secure the Vessel, instead of pursuing the Offenders.[15]

The idiom of this analogy is suitably heroic, but when dealing with Whig madness, Swift adopts a 'vulgar' but witty conceit:

> A DOG loves to turn round often; yet after certain *Revolutions*, he lies down to *Rest*: But Heads, under the Dominion of the *Moon*, are for perpetual *Changes*, and perpetual *Revolutions*: Besides, the

Whigs owe all their Wealth to *Wars* and *Revolutions;* like the Girl at *Bartholemew-Fair*, who gets a Penny by turning round a hundred Times, with Swords in her Hands.[16]

At their best, Swift's articles are distinguished by a style which makes his task seem like a sporting pleasure, in which he is sure of his integrity and ability. The Whigs, he seems to say, are such a farcical set of hypocrites that the best method seems to be the avoidance of serious analysis altogether.

This arrogant confidence often leads to a kind of rhetorical brinkmanship where we watch Swift deliberately provoking the Whigs and courting revenge. In one of the articles, he faces the obvious question of what will happen to him 'if Times should alter'. With calm indifference, he welcomes the prospect and, with taunting irony, says he expects 'to be a Favourite' whose present accusations will be entirely vindicated, provided the Whigs have the honesty to admit he was right. It is tempting to see Swift's bravado as either incredible naivety or else the result of acquired but genuine conviction. Part of it may be explained by the requirements of rhetoric, but it is doubtful whether such aggressive confidence could result from anything less than total commitment.

Certainly, Swift had little pity for writers doing his kind of work for the other side. Although he never once mentions Addison and Steele, his general lumping together of Whig 'hacks' must have, indeed did, alienate and enrage them. Swift, having convinced himself of the purity of his mission, found their reaction a bit peevish. In one of his last articles for the *Examiner*, knowing how provocative he had been to other writers, he made a point of brazenly dismissing their loyalties and status:

> For my own particular, those little barking Pens which have so constantly pursued me, I take to be of no further Consequence to what I have writ, than the scoffing Slaves of old, placed behind the Chariot, to put the General in Mind of his Mortality; which was but a Thing of Form, and made no Stop or Disturbance in the Show. However, if those perpetual Snarlers against me, had the same Design, I must own they have effectually compassed it; since nothing can well be more mortifying, than to reflect, that I am of the same Species with Creatures capable of uttering so much Scurrility, Dulness, Falshood and Impertinence, to the Scandal and Disgrace of Human Nature.[17]

This must be one of the most savage concessions in literature. With seeming indifference to the possibility of a reversal in his situation, and that of his masters, Swift seems to be trying to write the Whigs out of history. Although he claimed never to indulge in *ad hominem* abuse, he had included several ruthless pieces on famous individuals, including the Duke of Marlborough, General of the English army in Europe, and Thomas Wharton, ex-Lord Lieutenant of Ireland, now on the Whig front bench.[18] A surgical relish went into the composition of these pieces, in the belief that individual characters, precisely because of their power and reputation, deserved special punishment. This was to prove, in a very short time, a regrettable miscalculation: people remembered the slander not the ideal. Also relevant to the personalised nature of these attacks is Swift's understanding of history as the burden and legacy of individual personalities, rather than any more impersonal analysis of social, economic and political forces.

The propaganda which Swift produced for the *Examiner* gives us a specific example of the special relation between ideology and talent which he believed resulted in effective writing. When he characterises these counter-attacks as 'Dulness, Falshood and Impertinence', he points to their beliefs as well as to their lack of talent, insisting that the former explains the latter. For Swift, a hopeless cause is bound to produce bad writing. This, he would argue, is a fact not a prejudice. The several literary talents among the Whigs are frustrated by the absurdity of their position, while a great cause such as a Tory scheme for peace encourages clarity and insight:

> ... Men of a great Genius are hardly brought to prostitute their pens in a very odious *Cause*: which, besides, is more properly undertaken by Noise and Impudence, by gross Railing and Scurrility, by Calumny and Lying, and by little trifling Cavils and Carpings in the wrong Place, which those *Whifflers* use for Arguments and Answers.[19]

Swift can afford such condescension not because his argument is reasonable, but because of his superior talent and the confidence, inspired by power, which it exudes. In an important sense, he is absolutely correct to insist that faith and conviction are the foundation of a great style.

Finally, we should not neglect the influence of satisfied ambition in this polemical crusade. Swift was now the darling of a ruling party. He had been writing, mostly anonymously, for over ten years, and must have felt that he was finally showing the literary world how it should be done. The tactic of facelessness was by now almost a habit, more suited to style than reality, since everyone could observe Swift's political and social company. This sense of defiant elation is heard in one of his *Examiner* pieces, written in February 1711, when he addresses those Whig writers who suspect his identity:

> They have in their Prints openly taxed a most ingenious Person as Author of it; one who is in great and very deserved Reputation with the world, both on Account of his Poetical Works, and his Talents for publick Business. They were wise enough to consider, what a Sanction it would give their Performance, to fall under the Animadversion of such a Pen; and have therefore used all the Forms of Provocation commonly practiced by little obscure Pedants, who are fond of distinguishing themselves by the Fame of an Adversary.[20]

This image of genius surrounded by parasitical mediocrity dates back to the satire in *A Tale Of A Tub*. But, on this occasion, Swift is congratulating himself behind the protective screen of impartiality. His withering contempt for all competitors suggests the hard-won satisfaction of the successful outsider proving a talent which others had either begrudged or denied.

We can observe Swift, in the *Journal* for this period, looking back over his shoulder to Ireland for discreet congratulations on his new-found status. He mentions the *Examiner* regularly when talking about his new political friends in the Ministry, but never once admits that he is the author. Writing at the end of November, soon after he began the job, he is as cagey as ever:

> But, to say the truth, the present ministry have a difficult task, and want me, &c. Perhaps they may be just as grateful as others: but, according to the best judgement I have, they are pursuing the true interest of the public; and therefore I am glad to contribute what is in my power. For God's sake, not a word of this to any alive.[21]

Pride struggles with prudence throughout this correspondence. In

December, he urges Stella to get copies of the *Examiner*, and adds,
'. . . the great men assure me they are all true. They are written by
their encouragement and direction.' Later, pleased she liked them,
Swift still persisted in the innocent deceit, 'Nobody knows who it
is, but those few in the secret, I suppose the ministry and the
printer.' Even during the week when he wrote his final contribution, he could not resist a broad hint: 'As for *The Examiner*, I have
heard a whisper, that after that of this day, which tells what this
parliament had done, you will hardly find them so good. I
prophecy they will be trash for the future.'[22] The *Journal* has an
important, confessional relation to his political writing, and it
establishes a fascinating contrast of manner and disguise. The
faceless role of the *Examiner* is Swift's *doppelgänger*, flushed with
excitement, success and power: in the *Journal*, we listen to the
writer off duty, so to speak, looking for reassurance from someone
he loves and misses.

Some of Swift's triumphalism in these articles may, quite understandably, be linked to the appearance of his *Miscellanies in Prose
and Verse*, published in February 1711, half-way through his stint as
Tory propagandist. This anonymous volume brought together
Swift's writings from the previous decade, a project he had been
planning long before his present position. Now that his political
allegiance seemed to have been transferred from Whig to Tory, the
content and presentation of the *Miscellanies* required special diplomacy. Even before coming over to England, Swift had written to
the printer, Benjamin Tooke, preparing the ground for avoiding
any political embarrassment:

> I would not have you think of Steele for a publisher: he is too
> busy. I will, one of these days, send you hints, which I would
> have in a preface, and you may get some friend to dress them
> up. I have thoughts of some other work one of these years; and I
> hope to see you ere it be long; since it is like to be a new world,
> and since I have the merit of suffering by not complying with the
> old.[23]

Put bluntly, Swift could foresee that it would be against his own
interests to identify himself and his work with Steele and the
Whigs, while seeking favours from a new administration. Before
publication, Swift carefully revised part of the *Contests and Dissensions* (a section which implied a link between bribery at elections

and a Tory success in 1698), and added a preface to the *Letter Concerning the Test*, which points out its principled stand against Whig moves for Toleration. After much politic trimming, the volume was handed over to Tooke who, on Swift's advice, printed it with another publisher's name, John Morphew, on the title-page. This subterfuge was used to cover his tracks because Tooke had published the fifth edition of the *Tale*: if his name appeared with the *Miscellanies*, the author could be deduced. It seemed to escape Swift's notice that, since Morphew also published the *Examiner*, an alternative deduction could be made.

The *Miscellanies* appeared on 27 February 1711, and the following day Swift wrote in the *Journal*:

> Some bookseller has raked up every thing I writ, and published it t'other day in one volume; but I know nothing of it, 'twas without my knowledge or consent; it makes a four shilling book, and is called *Miscellanies in Prose and Verse*. Tooke pretends he knows nothing of it, but I doubt he is at the bottom. One must have patience with these things; the best of it is, I shall be plagued no more. However, I'll bring a couple of them over with me for MD, perhaps you may desire to see them. I hear they sell mightily.[24]

Swift's authorial coyness is often quite amusing since he was one of London's best-known writers. Retaining the fiction of innocence and detachment does have a certain political and legal justification, but it is hard to see why it survives for so long in the *Journal*. As with the *Examiner*, Swift regularly pestered Stella with questions about the *Miscellanies*, keeping up the charade for months. Even as late as the summer, he is surprised and, I think, a bit vexed, that she has not yet seen or read his collection. The world's judgement he could either welcome or defy, but the instant approval of a loved one remained a playful obsession.

Although Swift wrote his last contribution to the *Examiner* in early June, he was not yet free to return to Ireland. Pleased by his new prestige as a political commentator, he had still to attend to the original business of the First Fruits. After nine months, this issue was formally agreed but, as Swift had observed with the Whigs, politicians usually arranged favours to suit their own political strategy. Throughout the summer of 1711, Swift wrote repeatedly to Archbishop King, reassuring him that the negotiations were under control but complaining of the tardy and devious habits of politicians. Similar complaints characterise nearly every letter to Dublin. His frustration is quite genuine, although it can sometimes sound like a pleasurable effect of his new sense of importance – 'I long to be in Ireland; but the ministry beg me to stay.' The truth was more complicated, since without taking advantage of the influence of his new masters, he could not hope for any clerical promotion. This image of himself as a dutiful and patriotic writer, happy to serve but yearning for a simpler, domestic retreat is a central motif in the *Journal*, an ambiguous fiction which outlived his stay in England, and which holds within itself many of the contradictory forces in Swift's literary personality.

Swift was by now what might be termed a 'kept' writer, who had to endure long periods of simply waiting for news of his negotiations or instructions for new publications. To some extent, his literary timetable was ordered by parliamentary and ministerial activity. In the summer of 1711, he followed his political friends and masters for weekends at the Court of Windsor. Here, surrounded by aristocracy and royalty, Swift tried to live up to the image of wealth and sophistication which such an exquisite residence seemed to require, but his correspondence to Stella gives us the farce as well as the glory. His notorious servant, Patrick, regularly turned up drunk, or disappeared for days. When Swift could not catch a lift from London to Windsor with friends like the Lord Treasurer, he cursed the expense of such outings. Musical evenings at the Court tortured him almost as severely as the summer heat. Being a Court-follower was an expensive and idle experience, something totally unsuited to Swift's temperament.

The energy and variety of cosmopolitan London offered Swift many compensations while he was waiting for news or work. He enjoyed visiting the many coffee-houses and bookshops, yet dreaded the cost. These outings became almost a sinful pleasure for someone who daily noted every farthing spent. Paying out several pounds for a couple of books filled him with horror and delight. One day he attended an auction of rare, antiquarian books, and later that evening wrote to Stella, '. . . I itch to lay out nine or ten pounds for some fine editions of fine authors. But 'tis too far, and I shall let it slip, as I usually do all such opportunities.' A fortnight later, the temptation is too much – '. . . I went to the auction of Barnard's books, and laid out three pounds three shillings, but I'll go there no more; and so I said once before, but now I'll keep to it.' For someone as parsimonious as Swift, who refused to light a fire until 1 November, no matter what the weather, money spent on his library was a painful but vital indulgence. By mid-summer, he informed the ladies, 'My library will be at least double when I come back.' After this letter, he had two more years of temptation before everything was shipped back to Dublin.

Swift's literary friendships underwent political changes during this period, since he was now a writer who refused to separate the interests of literature and politics. He no longer socialised with Addison and Steele, justifying the break in this literary friendship in terms of Whig ingratitude and Tory appreciation:

> I never see them, and I plainly told Mr Harley and Mr St John, ten days ago ... that I had been foolish enough to spend my credit with them in favour of Addison and Steele; but that I would engage and promise never to say one word in their behalf, having been used so ill for what I had already done.[25]

This *mea culpa* is one of those very rare moments when we hear Swift record any form of apology: within the privacy of the *Journal*, this is perhaps not surprising, but it also shows his more character-istic defiance of literary opposition.

His scorn for his old associates is understandable if we appreci-ate the range and character of Swift's new literary circles. The week after he finished with the *Examiner*, he became a member of a literary club founded by St John, called simply 'The Society', which was conceived as a Tory élite of statesmen and writers which would both dignify and serve that political interest. Swift ex-plained the scheme to Stella:

> The end of our Club is to advance conversation and friendship, and to reward deserving persons with our interest and recom-mendation. We take in none but men of wit or men of interest; and if we go on as we begin, no other Club in this town will be worth talking to.[26]

The competitive nature of the plan, partly designed to outdo the Whig Kit-Kat club, gives us a sense of the political and social structure of literary activity in London at the time. It is like a freemasonry of taste, with patronage as a benevolent but guiding interest. Curiously, apart from Swift and Matthew Prior, most members of 'The Society' were politicians and statesmen, not writers.

It is typical of Swift's literary energy that, while living the outward life of a courtier, patiently waiting for preferment, he should be working on artistic projects more to his personal taste and inclination than the rhetorical polemics required by the ministers. During the relatively idle months following the *Examiner*, he resurrected the idea of an academy which would regulate and systematise changes in the English language, a proposal already sketched in the *Tatler*, the previous September. 'The Society' obviously represented an embryonic form of such an academy. Writing in the *Journal*, he envisages Harley as the financial patron of '. . . a society or academy for correcting and settling our language, that we may not perpetually be changing as we do.' This was always one of Swift's literary dreams, although it never materialised. He kept his notes for such a project, hoping to promote the ideas at some later, more opportune, time.

As the government's chief writer, confidant of the Ministry, member of 'The Society', a familiar face at Court, and regular guest at the tables of London's upper classes, Swift soon discovered his own powers of patronage, which he usually dispensed with charity and acumen. For example, he took special care to secure financial aid for Congreve, who was in very poor health, by urging his case personally with Harley. He also spoke for friends of Stella who had arrived in London looking for some respectable employment. Within literary circles, he was now able to influence the fortunes of some of London's principal publishers and printers. For example, he helped Benjamin Tooke and John Barber obtain printing rights for the *Gazette*, the government paper. He was ready to repay their efficiency and discretion with several lucrative appointments and sinecures. A trustworthy relationship with a reliable publisher was vital to a writer like Swift who courted so much political controversy and legal retaliation.

Swift undertook two pamphlets towards the end of the summer of 1711, both prompted by England's secretive attempts to obtain a separate peace settlement with France over the protracted war. Because of the political sensitivity of the issue, Swift had to exercise special care in shielding his identity. Although the two pamphlets illustrate perfectly his habitual separation of playful and serious styles, the one a *jeu d'esprit*, the other an exercise in political persuasion, they are both essays in literary stealth. They also show us the crucial importance of a trustworthy publisher in such intrigues, whose role was much more active than we might expect.

The first of these pamphlets was *A New Journey to Paris*, an ironic prank conceived in late August. It was inspired by the public scandal over Matthew Prior who, acting as a clandestine negotiator for the government, had visited France to discuss a possible treaty. Such a unilateral move angered many people who considered it a betrayal of England's allies, especially of Holland. Swift moved quickly to counter the government's embarrassment over what looked like an unpatriotic and shady affair. He told Stella of his idea for salvaging Prior's reputation and the Tories' image: 'I will make a printer of my own sit by me one day, and I will dictate to him a formal relation of Prior's journey, with several particulars, all pure inventions, and I doubt not but it will take.'[27] Within a week, Swift had indeed dictated a fictitious account of the journey, supposedly written by a French attendant present at the negotiations, and quickly translated into English. The spurious revelation cleverly emphasised Prior's patriotism and honour by recalling his hostility and arrogance towards his French hosts. Swift's knowledge of French helped authenticate the bogus narrative. To play down the significance of Prior's status, the writer remembers him as 'a menial Servant', and certainly not a diplomat.

This short, twopenny pamphlet appeared on 11 September. Swift was invited that very evening to dine at Prior's home, an encounter he enjoyed relaying to Stella:

> ... when I came in Prior shewed me the pamphlet, seemed to be angry, and said, Here is our English liberty: I read some of it, and said I like it mightily, and envied the rogue the thought; for had it come into my head, I should have certainly done it myself.[28]

His secretive pleasure at the success of his fiction, especially keen when sitting beside its victim, was completed by its instant commercial popularity. It sold a thousand copies on the day of publication, doubling that figure within another week.

The other pamphlet which appeared soon after the skit on Prior, *The Conduct of the Allies*, was the 'bestseller' of Swift's career up to this point, although today it is almost forgotten. This was an altogether different kind of pamphlet, a solemn, lengthy piece of carefully planned propaganda required by the government to discredit the opposition and encourage popular support for its efforts to arrange a separate peace with France. There was no place here for jokes, irony or trickery. A job of serious persuasion was in order: the manner had to be suitably rigorous and elevated, but aggressive and partisan. This commission was Swift's greatest rhetorical challenge while serving the Tories: he was now entrusted with the task of speaking for England's role in international affairs.

The Conduct of the Allies was not Swift's idea, but part of government strategy. The timing of its appearance, as with all controversial pamphlets, was almost as important as its content. Oxford and St John approached Swift during August, told him what was needed, supplied him with privileged information about diplomacy and finance, and urged him to have the pamphlet ready for the opening of parliament in November. Paradoxically, Swift showed little enthusiasm for a work which would almost certainly crown his literary service to the Tories. In the *Journal*, several cautious allusions to this enterprise sound weary rather than excited, as if he now realises that he is being exploited. In late August he wrote:

> There is now but one business the ministry wants me for; and when that is done, I will take my leave of them. I never got a penny from them, nor expect it. In my opinion, some things stand very ticklish; I dare say nothing at this distance.[29]

Since defending Tory policy inevitably meant slandering the Whigs, the pamphlet required a doctrinal manner and a partisan edge which, I think, had been somewhat exhausted by the *Examiner*. But Swift was very determined to lead the assault on the Whigs, and noted, 'I'll cool them, with a vengeance very soon.' As a writer, Swift had never enjoyed so little control over a piece of work: for nearly three months, he researched and drafted versions of the pamphlet under the careful supervision of St John, who was chiefly responsible for supplying facts and figures for the arguments. On 10 November, he told Stella:

> Why; if you must have it out, something is to be published of great moment, and three or four great people are to see there are no mistakes in point of fact: and 'tis so troublesom to send it among them, and get their corrections, that I am weary as a dog.

I dined to-day with the printer, and was there all the afternoon; and it plagues me, and there's an end, and what would you have?[30]

Despite the grind of collaboration and supervision, Swift met the required deadline. At the end of November, he wrote that he had just finished the work 'which has cost me so much time and trouble'. It was being printed just in advance of the new parliamentary session which would debate those very issues already set out in the pamphlet.

It was published on 27 November, priced at a shilling a copy, and was sold out on the same day.[31] A second edition appeared two days later, disappeared in five hours, and a third edition, which required that the printers work on Sunday, sold out in two days. Harley, watching its reception closely, advised a couple of alterations for a fourth edition which appeared in early December and sold out immediately. This was the last edition which Swift personally supervised. A fifth edition, in smaller print, costing sixpence, was published at the end of the month, and sold four thousand copies. When the sixth edition did the same in January, the pamphlet had sold a phenomenal eleven thousand copies.

The extraordinary popularity of *The Conduct of the Allies* is hard to appreciate today, since it seems such an unlikely piece by someone famed for satire. Its contemporary interest lay in its confident and comprehensive case for peace, a demand reinforced by what must have seemed a limitless and fluent command of inside information.[32] The anonymous author seems to know the history of European diplomacy backwards, always maintaining a dignified but plain style, occasionally using technical and legal terms to impress, and arguing with unhesitating conviction that the interests of England and Tory policy are identical. The only deviation from this largely positive appeal is the predictable attack on the 'former ministry', which Swift characterises as a 'monied interest' bent on continuing war for private financial gain. This simple but potent distinction between the public interest of a nation and the private greed of individuals is the main rhetorical device of the pamphlet, without which its historical knowledge would sound like mere pedantry. Swift got the balance between moral idealism and political sophistication just right.

The same was true of the pamphlet's timing. Before parliament could debate the issues, it looked as if the Tories had already made

a clear, decisive case. The pamphlet had both caught the Whigs off
guard, and effectively determined the political agenda. When the
debate actually got under way, Swift was delighted to see many
MPs using his pamphlet for ideas and arguments. He noted
gleefully, 'The noise it makes is extraordinary.' But tactical advantage and political controversy ensured neither security nor success
for Swift. The Whigs moved quickly to prosecute the printer, John
Morphew, and force him to name the author. In his *Journal*, Swift
begins to sound extremely nervous about these legal proceedings,
and hopes that Morphew 'will stand to it, and not own the author;
he must say, he had it from the penny-post.' Swift also knew that if
the Tories were defeated in parliament, he would soon be at the
mercy of a new administration. Morphew was brought before a
Lord Chief Justice, interrogated and threatened with imprison-
ment, but soon released with a warning. Swift seriously considered
foreign exile, just in case the pamphlet and the debate which it
intensified were to backfire. Slanderous accusations, he quickly
realised, could work both ways. His fetish of literary anonymity
was now irrelevant, since he was usually, and accurately, blamed
for stylish slanders against the Whigs. Reputation could be an
annoyance: 'But I would be out of the way upon the first of the
ferment; for they lay all things on me, even some I have never
read.'[33] Swift's affected invisibility was becoming farcical, since the
whole of London was pointing at him, while he pretended not to
exist. His nervous dread was soon allayed, however, as the Queen
appointed twelve new Lords at the end of December to ensure a
Tory majority. After a bad fright, Swift was now ecstatic and safe.

For the first time since he had come to England, over a year
before, he understood that, by attaching himself as a writer to the
volatile world of party politics, he had made an irrevocable
decision. Much as he would continue to lament the viciousness of
party scheming and wrangling, or to regret the tranquillity of
Laracor, he was no longer an independent writer. Ambition
required a pact with power. His writing now seemed dominated by
that very factionalism he had once satirised as the source and
symptom of civic madness. Even before the crisis sparked off by
the pamphlet, Swift confessed his dilemma:

But I am kept here by a most capricious fate, which I would
break through, if I could do it with decency or honour. – To
return without some mark of distinction would look extremely

little; and I would likewise gladly be somewhat richer than I
am.[34]

Principled loyalty without payment was a pleasing but difficult
self-image to sustain. Self-interest, whenever tactfully opportune,
was in desperate need of satisfaction.

Swift's obsession with this political crisis extended beyond its
temporary resolution, and shows how he continued to understand
this phase in terms of the personalities involved. In his view, all
such crises were explicable as a titanic battle between individual
virtue and evil. Genuinely believing that his 'independent' position
as a writer at court ensured an understanding denied to his
political allies, he continued to write in the hope that he could
influence events by clarifying the essential personalities of the
main actors in the drama. He first singled out the Earl of Nottingham, a Tory who had decided to vote with the Whigs against the
peace treaty, and lambasted him in 'An Excellent New Song', a
scurrilous and largely ineffective broadside. Warming to his old
penchant for poetic assassination, he then turned to the Duchess
of Somerset, a lady at Court who Swift believed was personally
influencing the Queen against the ministers. He drafted a mock-
prophecy, written in Gothic black-letter, had it copied 'in an
unknown hand', and published it as a genuine prophecy of
Somerset's betrayal of the monarchy. As so often with his verse,
Swift was delighted with the deceit, so much so that he even
introduced it openly to his Society gathering, which ensured that
the original secrecy was lost. He remarked in the *Journal* 'I like it
mightily,' and rather ingenuously concluded, 'I believe everybody
will guess it to be mine, because it is somewhat in the same manner
with that of *Merlin* in the *Miscellanies*.' Swift always seemed to
imagine that personal slanders, when conducted through playful
verse, would never be held against him, that they were somehow
more innocent than attacks in prose. This was to be a mistake, for
his enemies included everything in their tally.

For a few months more, the peace negotiations continued to
dominate Swift's writings. In January 1712, he became alarmed at
the rising discontent from the extreme right of the Tory party,
known as 'The October Club'. These Tories were as violently
anti-Whig as Swift, but were now criticising Oxford's slow resolution of negotiations and his reluctance to punish Whig critics. For
Swift, this was a most unprecedented and difficult kind of dissent,

one which confused his usual understanding of loyalty and treachery. He took it upon himself to reassure them, in an anonymous pamphlet entitled *Some Advice to the October Club*. As with so many of his writings on this issue, the content retains little direct interest today, since the arguments were restricted to a minor and passing question of tactics. But the preparation of the pamphlet, and Swift's response to its reception, show us a dimension of his literary career rarely acknowledged.

He first wrote out the pamphlet himself, then had his friend Charles Ford make out a copy in his own handwriting, which was then sent to a printer. When it appeared, on 21 January, Swift dined with the printer, John Morphew, who showed him the work without knowing he was speaking to the author. Swift told Stella, 'I commended it mightily; he never suspected me.' The pamphlet is a very polished exercise in respectful and flattering appeal. It does not rely solely on a civil request for loyalty in difficult times, but makes clear that the pamphlet comes 'from no mean Hand, nor from a Person uninformed'. It reassures its audience by impressing it with confidential hints that such fears are respected, and that impatience is understandable but unworthy. It has the skilled manner of a benevolent and seasoned statesman, gently reprimanding those who suffer a temporary loss of direction. Knowing how panicky Swift had become, such stylistic assurance is a mark of his imaginative resourcefulness.

Unlike everything else he had written on the war and negotiations for peace, this pamphlet attracted little interest. Vexed at its poor showing, Swift managed to find some principled consolation:

> I know not the reason; for it is finely written, I assure you, and, like a true author, I grow fond of it, because it does not sell: you know that is usual to writers, to condemn the judgement of the world: if I had hinted it to be mine, everybody would have bought it, but it is a great secret.[35]

Commercial failure is happily interpreted as proof of its quality and integrity. It had been a long time since Swift had been able to indulge this sense of being 'a true author' who writes for himself and scorns popular acceptance or understanding. I think this is an expression of relief that such failure can restore his sense of independence and honesty as a writer. And yet that last line recalls his wounded vanity, which would love to shed all disguises and show the literary world its foolishness. In all his dealings with the Tories, Swift had tried to preserve the ideal of an independent witness, but the popularity of his tracts made such a principle seem more like nostalgia than fact: disappointment seemed an authentic emotion for 'a true author'.

Swift's *A Proposal for Correcting, Improving and Ascertaining the English Tongue*, which he had been nursing for over a year and finally published on 17 May 1712, shows clearly this insoluble contradiction between asserted freedom and necessary dependence. On the one hand, it is a familiar but closely argued case for an academy which would supervise and codify the present state of the language. Members would publish authoritative judgements on grammar, spelling and the acceptability of new, foreign words into learned discourse. Such a body, he pointed out, had already existed in France since 1635, where the language of learning and culture was more studiously protected than in England, and where artists could look to such an academy for financial support and political protection. On the other hand, Swift deliberately made this proposal into a piece of political flattery and opportunism, by addressing it personally to Oxford and shamelessly signing his name at the end. For all his scruples about the artistic dangers of too close a familiarity with power, this pamphlet shows that he was determined to share Oxford's political immortality.[36] For a pamphlet which could solemnly argue that the slavish spirit of a people reduces wit to 'Panegyric, the most barren of all Subjects', it is one of the most servile gestures Swift ever made.

Despite its occasional eccentricities, and its facile reductive explanations of racial and linguistic characteristics, the proposal deserves serious consideration as part of Swift's lifelong concern with language and style. It recognises that the English language is a hybrid, the effect of historical and political developments: such distinctive variety is in special need of scholarly attention. It also sees that the written and the spoken language of the Court is the strongest influence on writers attracted to that class. The general sobriety of this analysis is sometimes dropped when Swift dates the corruption of the language from the rise of Dissent in the mid-seventeenth century. Linguistic barbarism, it seemed, was yet another evil of non-conformity in religion and politics.

A more specific complaint is the absence of any agreement on the spelling of many words. (This orthographic confusion becomes one of Swift's favourite games with Stella in the *Journal*.) Some kind of grammatical dictionary was also required in the interest of conformity and clarity. Yet a classicist and traditionalist like Swift abhorred the idea, urged by many improvers, 'that we ought to spell exactly as we speak: which beside the obvious Inconvenience of utterly destroying our Etymology, would be a Thing we should never see an End of.' In one of the rare homely analogies of this otherwise academic exercise, he points out that such a reduction 'would be just as wise as to shape our Bodies to our Cloathes and not our Cloaths to our Bodyes'. (Note the interchangeable 'i' and 'y'.) Swift also disliked the current fashion for jargon, cant and abbreviations, which had their place in Grub Street, but should never be tolerated in more serious discourse.

Overall, the proposal embodies a flexible conservatism, avoiding the extremes of downright intolerance or indiscriminate enthusiasm for novelty. Language, like the political process it reflected and expressed, required watchful and sensitive authority. Swift's only criterion for effective writing, one which permits the coexistence of many styles, is 'Simplicity, which is one of the greatest Perfections in any Language'.

It is a pity that the last few paragraphs drop this matter completely and begin a laboured enconium on Oxford himself, elevating him to a Medici of the Tory party. There is also an embarrassing element of self-seeking, barely disguised by the nod-and-wink manner:

> I have known, some Years ago, several Pensions given to particular Persons, (how deservedly I shall not enquire), any one of which, if divided into smaller Parcels, and distributed by the Crown to those who might, upon Occasion, distinguish themselves by some extraordinary Production of Wit or Learning; would be amply sufficient to answer the End. Or, if any such Persons were above Money, (as every great *Genius* certainly is, with very moderate Convenience of Life) a Medal, or some Mark of Distinction, would do full as well.[37]

While the proposal was being printed, Swift wrote in the *Journal*, 'I suffer my name to be put at the End of it, wch I nevr did before in my Life.' This is nearly true, but on this occasion vanity got the better of tact. When the proposal was published, a couple of 'Answers' appeared which ridiculed the scheme itself as well as the author's obsequiousness.[38] Swift wrote to Stella, complaining about the unnecessary fuss and, with brazen innocence, commented that the pamphlet contained 'no Politicks, but a harmless Proposall about the Improvement of the Engl. Tongue'. Then, rather petulantly, he added, 'I believe if I writt an Essay upon a Straw some Fool would answer it.' The attachment to the Tories was turning a bit sour, and Swift's private correspondence shows increasing frustration with the thankless task of literary service.

During the summer of 1712, Swift was relatively idle, and his writings during this lull, compared to the extended and intense activity of the previous year, are brief, desultory and malicious. Temporarily free from official writing, he composed a series of anonymous broadsides, hinting to Stella that 'Grubstreet has been very fruitful: pdfr has writt 5 or 6 Grubstreet papers this last week.' The first of these, the most earnest and restrained, was *A Letter to a Whig-Lord*, which appeared in early July. This was a seemingly disinterested appeal to moderate Whigs to support the Queen and the Constitution, and to forget the misleading and factious loyalties of party.

The other writings of this group employ Swift's old trick of ventriloquism. This is done by producing confidential letters, supposedly written by Whig statesmen, which betray a secret disloyalty. They work by a devious kind of irony, whereby the putative author always writes in the false assumption that only the recipient is privy to the conspiracy. This design can be intensified if the identity of the recipient exposes an unsuspected, therefore shocking, relationship. For example, Swift drafted *A Letter from the Pretender to a Whig-Lord*, in which King James congratulates the party for its continued disaffection, promising outlandish favours once restored to the throne of England. In *A Letter of Thanks from Wharton*, the Whig politician congratulates a Bishop whose writings were recently condemned as subversive. To broaden the slander, Swift makes Wharton speak on behalf of the Kit-Kat Club. One of Swift's most obsessive figures, Wharton compounds his subversiveness by tastelessness, praising the Bishop's witless and prosaic style of writing. In *A Hue and Cry after Dismal*, a pastiche of sensational journalism, the Earl of Nottingham (known as 'Dismal' for his saturnine features) is reported as being a spy in Dunkirk, dressed as a chimneysweep, but fortunately detected and arrested. Finally, Swift also composed an over-complicated verse-lampoon, 'Toland's Invitation to Dismal', an imitation of Horace, in which the Irish Presbyterian invites Nottingham to celebrate the anniversary of King Charles I's murder by republicans and free-thinkers.[39] None of these pieces is of enduring quality, except perhaps the attack on Wharton, which is a masterly work of imaginative libel. Ironically, thrifty Swift rushed through all these works in order to meet a deadline of 1 August, after which all pamphlets and small newspapers were to be taxed by a new Stamp Act, in order to suppress the proliferation of libellous and scanda-lous material.

Apart from letters, and the idea of a history of the Tory ministry, Swift wrote very little for the rest of this frustrating year. After two years loyal work, there was still no concrete assurance about a new post. A more personal reason for this suspension of his usual literary industry was recurring sickness. Swift suffered regular bouts of dizziness and nausea, as well as being tortured by shingles. Yet during this depression he made a remarkably self-critical comment on the way his writing had changed in character since working for the Tories: 'See how my Stile is altered by living & thinking & talking among these People, instead of my Canal & river walk, and Willows.'[40] Although he had become an outstand-ing journalist, propagandist and political commentator, it is as if he feels that one style has been sacrificed for another, inferior one. The phrase 'these People' also questions the success of Swift's adoption of a career within such narrow circles. He had, I believe, simply become tired of writing under these conditions.

Yet he immediately decided to take his literary leave of the Tories by planning a magisterial account of the period, entitled *History of the Four Last Years of the Queen*, a valedictory essay which aimed to justify everything his masters, but especially Oxford, had done for the Crown. He wrote in the *Journal*:

I am engaged in a long work, and have done all I can of it, and wait for some Papers from the Ministry for materialls for the rest, & they delay me as if it were a Favour I asked of them; so that I have been idle here this good while, and it happened in a right time, when I was too much out of order to study.[41]

Clearly, the politicians did not share Swift's enthusiasm for more publicity, and left the writer to go it alone. This became the most demanding of his self-imposed projects. In October, two months after he began researching his book, he wrote:

I toil like a horse, and have hundreds of letters still to read; and

squeeze a line perhaps out of each, or at least the seeds of a line
. . . I have about thirty pages more to write . . . which will be sixty
in print.[42]

The ministers' patronage of Swift, and the flattering intimacy
which he enjoyed, obviously did not include open access to all
correspondence. In fact, unknown to Swift, Oxford and St John
(the latter now raised to Viscount Bolingbroke) were in secret
negotiations with the Pretender. The prying historian could quickly become an embarrassment and a nuisance. Oblivious to all this,
Swift slogged away at his project, and by December had written
'130 Pages in folio to be printed, & must write 30 more, which will
make a large Book of 4s'. In February he confesses that the writing
has become a chore, '. . . I shall return with disgust to finish it, it is
so very laborious.' By the time he actually completed the work, in
mid-May, he was actively discouraged from publication. Peace in
Europe had been reached through the Treaty of Utrecht, it was
rumoured that the Queen was dying, and the political order looked
set for another upheaval. Swift's monumental work, intended as a
tribute to the men he had served so faithfully and diligently, and
also as proof of his ability as an historian, had arrived at a bad time.
The *History* was preserved in manuscript for nearly half a century,
and was finally published in 1758, thirteen years after Swift's
death.

During these months of labour with his *History*, Swift became
especially touchy about being interrupted in his study. He had to
suffer the attention of many people looking for literary advice and
favour. Being one of the best-known writers in London ensured
this unwelcome disturbance:

> I am plagued with bad Authors, Verse and Prose, who send me
> their Books and Poems; the vilest Trash I ever saw, but I have
> given their names to my man, never to let them see me.[43]

This little-known aspect of Swift's writing career, so well detailed
in the *Journal*, which shows us the reluctant critic beating off the
writer's admirers, often has a comical flavour. For example, he tells
of how he arrived home one evening to discover a parcel addressed to him: 'I had a present sent me . . . of the finest wild fowl I ever
saw, with the vilest Letter and from the vilest Poet in the World,
who sent it to me as a bribe to get him an Employment.'[44] Not

knowing the address of the sender, Swift gave away most of the lure, remarking on the ironic significance of the donation. '. . . the Rogue should have kept the Wings at least for his Muse.' Incidents like these remind us that the daily, anecdotal history of a writer like Swift, especially one serving the ruling party of a nation, gives us a dramatic and human sense of a writer's ordinary life, an effect rarely felt in most critical narratives. For this we must thank the *Journal*.

More elevated events, however, were on the horizon. Once the peace of Utrecht was formally signed and agreed, the Queen prepared to address Parliament. Oxford asked Swift to correct the draft of her speech, and to compose a formal resolution of thanks from the House of Lords. Swift took this invitation as a supreme honour, later hearing his own words spoken at the solemn ceremony.

Amidst the euphoria over the new peace, an important literary introduction was made to Swift: Alexander Pope, a rising young poetic talent, had just published *Windsor Forest*, celebrating the diplomatic achievement. The two writers met through a mutual friend, Lord Lansdowne, a member of Swift's 'Society'. Swift was delighted to see another writer praising what he considered a Tory victory, and urged Stella to read Pope's 'fine Poem'. After the peace, there was some relaxation of the social tensions within London's literary cliques, and Swift decided to hold a 'breakfast levee' for a group of friends and writers, including Addison, Steele and the newly arrived Irish cleric and philosopher, George Berkeley. In early April, the group was in turn invited by Addison to attend a rehearsal of his play, *Cato*, at Drury Lane. Swift's bored reaction to the proceedings is recorded in the *Journal*:

> . . . we stood on the Stage & it was foolish enough to see the Actors prompted every moment, & the Poet directing them, & the drab that acts Catos daughter out in the midst of a passionate Part, & then calling out, What's next?[45]

Theatre was always something of an imaginative blind-spot for Swift. On occasions like this, in the tense company of some former close friends, a willing suspension of disbelief proved impossible. Relations were much easier with new people like Berkeley, who Swift presented to the Court and the Ministers. Although Swift later described Berkeley's writings as 'too speculative',[46] he was

glad to help the young clergyman find his way in London's
political circles. Probably remembering his own arrival, he remarked to Stella that he felt it important 'to use all my little Credit
towards helping forward Men of Worth in the world'.

Berkeley's need also reminded Swift of his own plight. After
nearly three years in London, he was still the vicar of Laracor. The
First Fruits had been resolved in favour of the Church of Ireland,
but with no public recognition of Swift's crucial role. Politicians
like Oxford and Ireland's new Lord Lieutenant, the Duke of
Ormonde, squabbled over the credit for work patiently done by
Swift. At this point, no longer able to bear the suspense and
humiliation, he declared to Oxford that he was preparing to return
immediately to Ireland, unless some suitable English appointment
was offered. The gift of bishoprics lay ultimately with the Queen,
but deaneries could be decided by the Ministry. When several
vacancies appeared, Swift hoped his reward would be an English
bishopric. Instead, the Duke of Ormonde offered him the deanery
of St Patrick's Cathedral in Dublin, while Oxford suggested a
prebendary at Windsor. Swift was furious over this Hobson's
choice which fell way below his sense of just reward: '. . . I confess,
as much as I love Engld, I am so angry at this Treatment, that if I
had my Choice I would rather have St Patrick's.'[47] The polite world
of courtly patronage had become a cattle-market, with several
clerics, including Swift, jostling for attention and selection. It was
rumoured that the Queen, on the advice of the Duchess of
Somerset, had reconsidered the sanctity of the author of *A Tale Of
A Tub*, and was determined that Swift would never hold a
bishopric in England.[48]

After several excruciating days waiting for confirmation of his
new Irish post, Swift tried to preserve his dignity by a stoical
acceptance, glad that the bargaining was coming to a close. On 25
April 1713 he was officially declared Dean of St Patrick's, and
immediately started to pack, in order to arrive early for installation.
On 1 June, he set off from London, stayed at Chester for a couple of
days rest, exhausted from riding horseback for the first time in
almost three years. Here he wrote his sixty-fifth, and final, letter of
the *Journal*, telling the ladies to expect him in about a week. The
sullen return proved a false ending, as London had not yet finished
with him.

Stella, while reading of Swift's plans to return, was unaware that
he was simultaneously writing to another young woman, Esther

Vanhomrigh, with whom he had enjoyed a similar relationship. Miss Vanhomrigh, or 'Mishessy' as he called her, was the daughter of Mrs Bartholemew Vanhomrigh, widow of an ex-mayor of Dublin. Swift had met mother and daughter in London shortly after his arrival in 1710. His relationship with them was discreet and paternal. Even though he mentioned the women in his letters to Stella, he never acknowledged the kind of closeness which had developed between himself and the daughter.[49] Swift, thinking he was now leaving London for good, composed the longest poem he ever wrote, *Cadenus and Vanessa*, in which he playfully and self-critically reviewed the relationship, and tried to justify his disinclination to continue the affair.

This subjective narrative is framed around a mythological conceit whereby the gods, in their heavenly court of law, hear the appeals and complaints of earthly lovers.[50] Most of the poem allows Vanessa to air her case that, having been tutored by her fatherly friend Cadenus (a Latin anagram for Swift's new post), any closer ties of affection are rejected by her fatherly lover. The tribute to Vanessa's beauty and intelligence is matched by wonder at her object of affection:

> Vanessa, not in Years a Score,
> Dreams of a Gown of forty-four;
> Imaginary Charms can find,
> In Eyes with Reading almost blind.[51]

Old enough indeed to be her father, Cadenus pleads a lack of romantic vitality as reason for his shyness. The gods despair of such an eccentric rejection of young beauty. Venus, the Queen of Love, concludes that Cadenus, like most men, is a hopeless case. This easy-going, humorous self-portrait was held secretly by Swift for fourteen years, and was finally published in the *Miscellanies* of 1727, a joint-production with Pope.

Once he arrived in Dublin, Swift went straight to the rural backwater of Laracor, as if the capital would only remind him of the even greater metropolis he had left behind. The pasturelands of Meath must have seemed both a relief and a disappointment after the high drama of the last three years. He confided this mixed emotion in a letter to 'Mishessy':

I design to pass the greatest part of the time I stay in Ireland here in the Cabin where I am now writing, neither will I leave the Kingdom till I am sent for, and if they have no further service for me, I will never see England again: At my first coming I thought I should have dyed with Discontent, and was horribly melancholy while they were installing me, but it begins to wear off, and change to Dullness . . . I am now fitter to look after Willows, and to cutt Hedges than meddle with Affairs of State.[52]

Swift never admitted to being content in Ireland: after three years in London it would have sounded perverse and insular. Yet I think it is clear that he was genuinely glad to be free of political pressure while, at the same time, hoping he was not forgotten.

After only a few weeks retirement, he was suddenly beseiged by alarming correspondence from friends in London pleading with him to return and use his influence to heal a serious rift between Oxford and Bolingbroke which threatened to destroy the party. Because of the Triennial Act, new elections were called. With the Tories in crisis, it looked likely that a Whig ministry was imminent. For personal reasons, as much as political loyalty, Swift decided on a last, short visit to see how he could help. On 9 September, after being home for only three months, he was back in London.

Although there was strong political conviction behind this speedy return, there was also a genuine, uncomplicated pull of personal friendship for the Lord Treasurer. This devotion to Oxford inspired literary tribute, in both solemn and witty form. Having already dedicated the academy project to him, Swift now wrote two poems celebrating his patron and friend, as if to reassure him of unquestioning loyalty in a time of crisis.

The first of these, 'To Lord Harley, since Lord Oxford, on his Marriage', was occasioned by the marriage of Oxford's son. It is a wholly conventional prothalamion lauding the virtues of the young couple and, by implication, the genius of the groom's father. Swift's occasional verse, like his prose, can be either outstanding or merely competent: its quality often depends on the subject and his emotional commitment. 'To Lord Harley' is a readable but conventional piece of ceremonial praise. Interestingly, it was probably offered as a gift, since Swift never tried to publish it.

The companion-poem shows a very different use of the same literary impulse. Its pedantic title, 'Part of the Seventh Epistle of the First Book of Horace Imitated', is followed by an energetically colloquial version of a classical encounter between old friends. It tells how Oxford, coming home from Court, spots a familiar parson in the street, who turns out to be Swift. After some embarrassment, the Lord Treasurer invites him to dinner where, after a hearty evening, he makes Swift the new Dean of St Patrick's. After a trial period, Swift returns to London, fed up and broke, and begs to be restored to his former ease. After so many lampoons and satires whose style often suffered from excessive emotion or effort, this is one of Swift's most playful and confident verses. The self-portrait offers a witty and essential summary of his years with the Tories:

> No Libertine, nor Over-nice,
> Addicted to no sort of Vice;
> Went wher he pleas'd, said what he thought,
> Not Rich, but ow'd no Man a Groat:
> In State-Opinions a-la-Mode,
> He hated Wharton like a Toad;
> Had giv'n the Faction many a Wound,
> And libell'd all the Junta round;
> Kept company with Men of Wit,
> Who often father'd what he writ;
> His Works were hawk'd in ev'ry Street,
> But seldom rose above a Sheet:
> Of late indeed the Paper-Stamp
> Did very much his Genius cramp;
> And, since he could not spend his Fire,
> He now intended to Retire.[53]

Although Swift could and did write in a wide variety of verse forms and styles, the rhyming banter of tetrameter couplets, a deceptively 'natural' style, best suited his poetical wit. Unlike the other poem on Oxford, a private affair, this was published immediately, showing Swift's clear sense of literary discrimination.

It was not long before this poetical dalliance with Oxford was overtaken by a political controversy, conveniently presenting itself in personal terms, which reactivated Swift's old polemical instinct. He had been following Steele's articles in the *Guardian* which accused the Tories, and Oxford in particular, of delaying vital military treaties with France. His old adversary, wrongly assuming that Swift was still behind the *Examiner*, had confidently accused the new Dean of having a hand in these prevarications. Having just been elected as the MP for Stockbridge, Steele, full of his new importance, wrote an open letter to the Bailiff of Stockbridge, *The Importance of Dunkirk Consider'd*, which appeared on 22 September. This pamphlet accused the government of deliberately surrendering this strategic town. Swift decided to settle the personal as well as the political score. The honour of his friend, Oxford, was also in question. On 2 November, he published *The Importance of the Guardian Consider'd*, an anonymous corrective to Steel's presumption, written 'By a Friend of Mr St---le', and addressed to the Bailiff of Stockbridge.

Many of the political points made by Swift are either too dated or familiar to be of interest, but the literary strategy of the reply shows a new tone, born out of his hard-won experience with the Tories. Rather than deal earnestly with Steele's arguments, which he finds obscure and illiterate, he first concentrates on the character of this 'Brother-Scribler'. The manner is condescending and blunt:

> Mr Steele is Author of two tolerable Plays, (or at least of the greatest part of them)[54] which, added to the Company he kept, and to the continual Conversation and Friendship of Mr Addison, hath given him the Character of a Wit. To take the height of his Learning, you are to suppose a Lad just fit for the University, and sent early from thence into the wide World, where he followed every way of Life that might least improve or preserve the Rudiments he had got. He hath no Invention, nor is Master of a tolerable Style; his chief Talent is Humour, which he sometimes discovers both in Writing and Discourse; for after the first Bottle he is no disagreeable Companion.[55]

The malice of this character-sketch is all the more effective since it is written by 'A Friend' who smiles knowingly at Steele's pretentions to sophistication. This strategy, and the contemptuous humour it encourages, allow Swift to treat Steele as a mediocrity rather than a villain. Factual proof of Steele's superficiality as a writer is shown by the number of his short-lived enterprises with the *Tatler*, the *Spectator*, the *Guardian*, and lately, the *Englishman*. The 'Friend' laughs at Steele's transparent pseudonym of 'Ironside' and his tedious habit of 'filling up Nitches with Words before he has adjusted his Conception to them'. By the end of the letter, Steele is dismissed as a pitiful and confused pretender to knowledge and authority, a most unfortunate choice of MP, and an embarrassing friend.

Undaunted by Swift's attack, Steele, under the direction of leading Whigs, began to assemble material for a large pamphlet, entitled *The Crisis*, which would yet again challenge the government and question the integrity of its ministers. Rumours of Queen Anne's declining health prompted Steele to include the emotive issue of the succession to the Crown. The tract appeared on 19 January 1714, after much advance publicity. Swift rose to the challenge, but took his time, determined to deal his antagonist a final, comprehensive blow in this duel of the pamphleteers. On 23 February, Swift's *The Publick Spirit of the Whigs* appeared, with an ironic sub-title thanking the opposition for giving Steele another chance to disgrace himself publicly.

Swift continues and intensifies his contemptuous manner when reviewing this latest irritation, dividing his attention evenly between the content and the style. Like an exasperated schoolmaster faced with careless homework, he deliberately and disdainfully holds up specimens of its confused style in order to humiliate his victim. Steele, he concedes, is sometimes capable of clarity: '. . . provided he would a little regard the Propriety and Disposition of his Words, consult the Grammatical Part, and get some Information in the Subject he intends to handle.'[56] Swift deliberately avoids the content of *The Crisis* until the problem of its illiteracy is appreciated. He even considers abandoning any attempt to unravel the knot of falsehoods and absurdities, but feels that the public interest requires the loathsome task. He then goes on to correct Steele's grammar, expose endless obscurities and careless ambiguities, laugh at Steele's misunderstanding of classical allusion, accuse him of treasonable talk, and dismiss this production by 'a Child of Obscurity' as entirely unoriginal. Exhausted by his effort to read the unreadable, Swift mockingly surrenders: 'A Writer with a weak Head, and a corrupted Heart, is an over-match for any single Pen, like a hireling Jade, dull and vicious, hardly able to stir, yet offering at every Turn to kick.'[57] Then, having systematically countered only those parts of the text which are comprehensible, he concludes, 'I have now finished the most disgustful Task that ever I undertook.' Although the length of Swift's reply undermines its dismissive tone, *The Publick Spirit of the Whigs* is one of his most accomplished and deadly exercises in derision. It makes no elaborate use of masks or ironical tricks: this is Swift's own voice, learned, witty and assured.[58] He is determined to give the opposition, through the pitiful example of Steele, a resounding lesson in the art of stylish polemic. The royal pamphleteer, we are made to feel, has just dealt with an incompetent pretender.

Swift may have won the literary duel, but he looked set to lose a legal case prepared against his pamphlet. The Whigs, understandably outraged by Swift's remarks about treasonable talk, brought the publishers, Morphew and Barber, before a committee of the House of Lords. Without openly declaring the identity of the author, they had to be released from custody. Swift and the printers were now very alarmed, and the second edition of the pamphlet appeared without the offending passages. In one of these passages, Swift, with his customary loathing for all things Scottish, had vilified that country's members in the House, calling them 'a fierce poor northern people'. Wharton started a petition to discover the author, which resulted in a royal proclamation offering three hundred pounds to anyone willing and able to reveal the man behind this 'seditious libel'. Amazingly, nobody claimed the reward, and a frightened Swift, who was previously one of the loudest defenders of such legislation, was relieved to see the matter die quietly. A final irony of this literary battle between the two Irishmen serving opposed English parties, took place in March. The Tories, having shielded Swift from Whig retribution, carried a motion in the House to expel Steele for his 'seditious papers'. The new MP for Stockbridge had lasted for one month, and was now disgraced: Swift had escaped the wrath of a law he actively supported.

This missionary return to England was dominated by these old political feuds, but it was also during this bitter period that he enjoyed the literary companionship of a select group of writers who shared his own playful, satirical sense of humour. He was now corresponding and meeting regularly with Pope, who had just published his version of Homer's *Iliad*. The witty intimacy between Pope, aged twenty-six, and Swift, aged forty-six, is reflected in a letter answering Swift's mock-proposal that the young poet convert to Protestantism for a reward of twenty guineas. After a series of solemn calculations on the price of faith, Pope reverses the invitation and appeals to 'Dr Swift, a dignified Clergyman, but one who, by his own Confession, has composed more Libels than Sermons'. Since 'too much Wit is dangerous to Salvation', he concludes that Swift 'must certainly be damned to all Eternity'. The joke is then transformed into a conceit for friendship:

... I should not think my own Soul deserved to be saved, if I did not endeavour to save his, for I have all the obligations in Nature to him. He has brought me into better Company than I cared for, made me merrier, when I was sick, than I had a mind to be, put me upon making Poems on Purpose that he might alter them, &.[59]

The letter concludes by telling Swift that the enlarged version of *The Rape of the Lock* is now ready for publication. Genuine friendship aside, having contacts with someone like Swift was an important part of young Pope's ambition.

Pope soon introduced his friend John Gay, poet and playwright, to the Dean. This company extended to include Dr Arbuthnot, the Queen's personal physician, and Parnell, clerical poet and a compatriot of Swift. Meeting in Arbuthnot's rooms at the palace, the group discussed plans for a mock-biography of one Martin Scriblerus, a caricature of intellectual pedantry. This group, as Ehrenpreis remarks, was the closest realisation of Swift's project for some kind of academy of wit. The Scriblerus circle never accomplished any shared work, although *Gulliver's Travels* (1725), *The Dunciad* (1728) and *The Beggar's Opera* (1728), represent the literary legacy of what began as a social gathering.

The Scriblerus Club was a pleasurable diversion and necessary escape from the bitter state of affairs in parliament. The Tory ministers and party were irrevocably divided, the Whigs were expecting a triumphant return to power, and the Queen was dying. No longer able or willing to embroil himself in political squabbles, Swift decided to leave London for good. Instead of going directly to Ireland, he went to stay with an old clerical friend, John Geree, in Letcombe Basset, Berkshire. On the last day of May 1714, having shipped six cases of his books to Dublin, he left for a period of privacy and reflection. He would not see London again for twelve years.

Swift regularly surprises us with his literary industry and energy. At this stage of the narrative, one would expect some kind of moratorium while he was enjoying the seclusion of rural Berkshire, free from the demanding grasp of London. On the contrary, Swift's output became quite frenetic, with endless letters written every day, a set of poems which reviews his recent past in London, a philosophical assessment of the political crisis, and notes for more historical prose.

In 'The Author Upon Himself', a poem in which he sketches his career at Court, he justifies and defends his personality:

> Swift had the Sin of Wit, no venial Crime;
> Nay, 'twas affirm'd he sometimes dealt in Rhime:
> Humour, and Mirth, had place in all he writ;
> He reconcil'd Divinity and Wit.[60]

A well-executed poem, it has a musical confidence matched perfectly by the flattering self-portrait of a man forced into early retirement by conspirators and fools. Another poem, an imitation of Horace, gives a more critical picture by contrasting rural sanity with urban oppression. Looking back on his reputation at Court, he feels that most people, especially the envious, exaggerated his influence and power. With echoes of the *Journal*'s longing for Laracor, he concludes:

> Thus in a Sea of Folly tost,
> My choicest Hours of Life are lost:
> Yet always wishing to retreat;
> Oh, could I see my Country Seat.
> There leaning near a gentle Brook,
> Sleep, or peruse some Antient Book;
> And there in sweet Oblivion drown
> Those Cares that haunt a Court and Town.[61]

Sounding more than ever like a stoical elder statesman playing the theme of *sic transit gloria mundi*, Swift shows his ability to command a convention rarely suited to his literary taste, but occasionally employed for a passing mood. This kind of adaptability is one of his greatest strengths as a writer. He published this reflective pastoral in 1727, but 'The Author Upon Himself', the more explosive of the two, was never published in his lifetime.

While in Berkshire, Swift also completed a contemplative analysis of the political crisis, *Some Free Thoughts Upon the Present State of Affairs*, which he had begun in London. Like the poems written in his rural hideaway, this essay affects a mature, sympathetic nostalgia for achievement betrayed and opportunity lost. Unlike the lively, personalised style of the verse, the prose is carefully impersonal and withdrawn in manner. The elegance and serenity of this patient reflection almost disguises a predictable and overworked argument. Put crudely, it contends that the ministers, through hesitation and toleration, have brought the current crisis upon themselves. Like a disillusioned and long-suffering civil servant who personally knew all the men behind the parliamentary rhetoric and scheming, he criticises the cult of secrecy and intrigue at the Court, a waste of talent better employed in stifling all opposition. The essay might well have been sub-titled 'Politics not a Mystery'. But how should a ruling party, during a crisis of confidence, deal with critical opposition? 'I take the Answer to be easy. In all Contests the safest way is to put those we dispute with, as much in the Wrong as we can.'[62] The irony of remarks like these lies in a contradiction easy for us to see, but one which did not exist for Swift. For him, there were never two sides to a question: in his defence of the 'natural' architects of England's political destiny, his obsession with all political forms of dissent led to a narrow sectarianism which seriously undermined the character of such essays, no matter how polished their style. The rhetoric is a pleasure, but the thuggery is again unmistakeable.

The story of Swift's attempts to publish *Some Free Thoughts*, while protecting its anonymity, is one of the most elaborate examples of his well-known mania for secrecy.[63] While the essay itself deplores 'this Mysticall manner of proceeding' in affairs of state, subterfuge and deception characterise every step towards its publication. Having written out a copy of his own, he got someone else, possibly his friend Geree, to make another copy. This copy, in unfamiliar handwriting, was sent by Swift to his friend Ford in London, asking him to fetch some passing porter off the street who would then be instructed to deliver it to the printer, Barber, without saying a word. The printer, completely innocent of the essay's origin, unfortunately passed the work to Bolingbroke, one of the central characters of the essay. The minister began to 'improve' the allusions to himself, but retained the criticisms of his rival, Oxford. Swift, waiting impatiently in the wings of this farce, sent another disguised copy, hoping it would be more acceptable, but still refused to declare ownership of the essay. After a long delay, he gave up the whole idea. In any event, when the Queen finally died on 1 August, such a pamphlet seemed inappropriate and irrelevant.

As so often with Swift's occasional writings, their effectiveness was wholly determined by events beyond the writer's control. Sometimes the timing was perfect, as with *The Conduct of the Allies*;

on other occasions, delays caused by secrecy and confusion made the work quickly redundant. Like yesterday's weather forecast, such writings died overnight. *Some Free Thoughts* suffered this fate, and was not published until 1741, when Swift's writing career was over.

The Queen's death was one of two calamities expected by Swift. The other, Oxford's dismissal, took place only days before the nation went into mourning. The two pillars of Swift's literary contribution to the period were now removed from a scene in which he made a final, desperate attempt to preserve his literary ties with England, while carrying on his clerical duties in Ireland. His various essays on contemporary history, combined with the latest exercises in political retrospection, made Swift feel as well qualified as any for the vacant post of Historiographer Royal. Shortly before the Queen died, he composed a dignified, but eager, memorial to the ailing monarch, to be delivered by her doctor, Arbuthnot, in which he offered himself for the prestigious post:

> ... it is necessary, for the honour of the Queen and in justice to her servants, that some able hand should be immediately employed to write the history of her Majesty's reign; that the truth of things may be transmitted to future ages, and bear down the falsehood of malicious pens.[64]

Not very surprisingly, the Queen decided that the Irish Dean, an ex-propagandist for a party whose leaders were secretly dealing with the Pretender, a libellous writer who had attacked many of her closest associates and friends, would not suit the requirements of the job. Disappointed but defiant, Swift decided that enough was enough. After several letters of farewell, including one to Oxford, and a weekend of diversion with Pope and Parnell, Swift headed north for Chester and Holyhead, arriving back in Dublin on 24 August.

Including a short interlude in Ireland, Swift had devoted almost four years of his literary energy to the Tory administration. It had been the most productive and demanding period of his career. From relative obscurity as a vicar employed by his Church on minor diplomatic business, he had enjoyed the patronage and friendship of the English ruling class. Because of this alliance, and despite his games of literary disguise, he was now one of the best-known writers in England. Apart from the *Journal* to Stella, however, his writings from this period are amongst his least-read works. Swift showed how he could write for any occasion, often under extraordinary pressure and without exclusive control over his productions. He proved that controversy and even propaganda required style if it was to be effective and popular, that the rhetoric of persuasion demanded consistency, authority and absolute conviction. But the original loyalty and determination became a kind of paranoia which narrowed rather than enlarged his imagination. In *Some Free Thoughts* he had remarked that 'some People may think perhaps I have already said too much.' It is a pity that he did not notice this excess sooner. To admire Swift's style in this period, as a thing apart, is reasonable and edifying; but the argument and morality of many of the Tory tracts had become predictable and jaded.

Placing this period in the broader perspective of Swift's writing career, I would suggest that it served as his second, and more decisive, apprenticeship. If he had not experienced this intimacy with power and the rhetorical strategies used to serve as well as to hide its interests, he could never have achieved his later, much-deserved reputation as a 'Hibernian patriot' who confronted English rule in Ireland. As Dean and Drapier, free of political patronage and control, free to exercise his rhetorical craft in the service of a wider, 'national' cause, Swift finds an ideal collusion between style and subject.

4

A Deceptive Retirement

A literary moratorium descended upon the new Dean of St Patrick's for the next six years. Although he continued to mull over the history of the Tory party, and wrote some private, occasional verse, he published nothing between 1714 and 1720, claiming depression, ill health and indifference as the causes for his silence. Reading his correspondence during this period, it is as if the imaginative element of Swift's character has been buried, while the clerical personality resigns itself to a lonesome retirement. Now approaching fifty years of age, Swift creates a self-portrait, in verse and letters, of a once-happy man condemned to live out his remaining years in a barbarous island from which he had earlier escaped.

A couple of months after his return, he wrote a short, mournful poem on his condition, entitled 'In Sickness', in which this sense of isolation is indulged to a sentimental extreme:

> 'Tis true, – then why should I repine,
> To see my Life so fast decline?
> But, why obscurely here alone?
> Where I am neither lov'd nor known.
> My state of Health none care to learn:
> My Life is here no Soul's Concern
> And, those with whom I now converse,
> Without a Tear will tend my Herse.[1]

Circumstances, in fact, were not quite as bad or as loveless. This is the expression of a mood, not the appreciation of changed company. Part of the explanation for Swift's relative silence during these years comes from his new post. No longer just a vicar, the new Dean had to learn the extent of his responsibilities and power, establish his authority within the Church's hierarchy, and devote much of his time and energy to the demanding routine of running his cathedral. He may not have wanted it, but he had become an important clergyman in the Irish Church.

Swift's cry of being a friendless recluse is, ironically, the dominant theme of a very active correspondence during these years.
Ignoring the closeness of his beloved Stella, and the arrival of
Vanessa, who so loved the Dean that she moved to Ireland to be
near him, Swift's complaint is directed to a wide variety of friends
left behind in England. Much of the news from England sounded
as depressing as Swift's own letters, but for different reasons. Once
returned to power, the Whigs began impeachment proceedings
against many leading Tories, including Oxford, and scrutinised the
correspondence of many of Swift's friends, such as Matthew Prior.
It was not a time to stand up for the Tory cause, especially when
figures like Bolingbroke, having fled to France, seemed to confirm
Whig accusations of Jacobitism. This political climate encouraged
both caution and paranoia, and must also be taken into account
when appreciating Swift's reserve.

The controversial pamphlets and satirical lampoons may have
ceased, but Swift remained a loyal and indefatigable writer of
letters. He wrote persistently to Oxford, even when the former
minister lay in the Tower of London, and reassured him of
unqualified support. Oxford rarely replied. Bolingbroke also received many letters from his old friend and supporter, replying
promptly from the safety of Paris. Swift's most regular correspondent, however, was his young friend, Charles Ford, to whom he
first voiced his stubborn misanthropy: 'I have been hindred by
perfect Lazyness, and Listelessness, and aneantissment to write to
You since I came here . . . I know not what to say to You. I cannot
think nor write in this Country.'[2] Swift still maintains a lofty
contempt for Ireland, as befits a man who had previously made it
to the top in England. This cultivated air of estrangement and
regret must have been reinforced when he read letters from his
English friends lamenting his absence and urging him to return.
His former printer, John Barber, kept him abreast of London's
political gossip, and added 'you are the reputed Author of every
good thing that comes out on our side.' Barber also warned Swift to
take special care of his writings, since the new government had
impounded letters in the Dublin and London post offices.[3] During
these years, Swift regularly kept in touch with Pope, whose literary
reputation was free of any political involvement. The former
company of Scriblerian friends like Pope was what Swift missed
most of all. He borrowed a copy of Pope's *Iliad* which, he told the
author, he 'read . . . in two evenings'. He enjoyed writing as a

friendly critic of the work, expressing his displeasure 'at some bad Rhymes and Triplets', but was delighted with the overall clarity of the verse, 'only in one or two places you are a little obscure'.[4] The young poet became an important literary confidant to the retired pamphleteer who wrote, 'you may truly attribute my silence to the eclypse', an allusion to Queen Anne's death and Swift's immediate leavetaking of England. He always asked Pope to pass on his regards to other literary friends, including Addison, Congreve, Rowe and Gay. He must have envied what he saw as Pope's freedom to write what and when he pleased. Years later he told him that poetry is 'an Art where Faction has nothing to do', and that being a pamphleteer by reputation meant he could never avoid partisan judgement of his work.[5]

In the summer of 1716, his old sense of parodic humour resurfaces when he writes to Pope recommending new material for a series of mock-pastorals:

> There is a young ingenious Quaker in this town who writes verses to his mistress, not very correct, but in a strain purely what a poetical Quaker should do, commending her look and habit, &c. It gave me a hint that a sett of Quaker-pastorals might succeed, if our friend Gay could fancy it, and I think it a fruitful subject; pray hear what he says. I believe further, the personal ridicule is not exhausted; and that a porter, foot-man, or chair-man's pastoral might do well. Or what think you of a Newgate pastoral, among the whores and thieves there?[6]

Determined not to be inspired by Ireland, his critical faculty often took the place of invention. It has been pointed out that the idea of a 'Newgate pastoral' probably led to Gay's *Beggar's Opera*,[7] and, as we shall see later, mock-pastoral becomes one of Swift's first literary exercises when he returns to writing poetry.

Swift's friendship with Matthew Prior offered him another opportunity to use his reputation to maintain literary links with London and, for the first time, establish them in Dublin. In January 1717, Erasmus Lewis, an old political ally and literary companion, wrote to Swift proposing the publication of Prior's verse in a special edition to be financed by generous subscriptions, the proceeds going directly to Prior, now in severe financial and political straits. Lewis asked Swift to act as literary agent for Prior in Ireland, and to seek out as many advance subscriptions as possible. Over the next two years, Swift put a great deal of work into this project, collecting pledges, remitting accounts to Prior's London publisher, writing endless begging-letters for the venture, arranging for the volume's distribution in Ireland.[8] This voluntary aid brought Swift into contact with Dublin's publishing world, where he was recommended the service of John Hyde. This printer handled all the work with Prior's volume, and seems to have done it so efficiently that Swift retained him for the first Dublin edition of *Gulliver's Travels* nearly a decade later. Reliable printers and publishers were, as we have seen earlier, a crucial part of Swift's literary career. He wrote to Pope during this period that he regarded them as 'Tools in my opinion as necessary for a good writer, as pen, ink and paper'. When they disappointed or crossed him, he saw them as a necessary evil. Besides introducing him to the publishing trade in Ireland, the task of collecting money from subscribers showed Swift the enormous difference in literary economy between the two countries. Always fastidious in money matters, he was tormented by people who subscribed and, once they received the book, pleaded poverty. The reading class in Ireland struck him as a beggarly lot compared to that of England.

In every way Ireland presented a shocking contrast to the England he had enjoyed and which he now constantly recalled in his letters. As late as December 1719, he wrote to Charles Ford complaining that the Irish climate prevented him from writing! More reasonably, his regular bouts of deafness and giddyness seem to account for much of his temporary inertia. He tells Ford, 'Thus in Excuse for my Silence, I am forced to entertain you like an old Woman with my Aylments,' and adds, miserably, 'You live in the midst of the World, I wholly out of it.' In the case of Bolingbroke's French exile, there was an opportunity to identify with a similarity of fate, despite the many contrasts of wealth and security. The exchanges between the two tell us as much about Bolingbroke's literary and philosophical pretensions as they reveal about Swift's pleasure in maintaining contact with the disgraced minister. Unlike others, Swift never hesitated to write to friends who were being watched closely by the authorities, sure of his own integrity and, in a perverse way, convinced that such disgrace was probable evidence of innocence. While Bolingbroke played the Stoic, Swift played the retired artist:

If you will recollect that I am towards six years older than when I saw you last, and twenty years duller, you will not wonder to find me abound in empty speculations: I can now express in a hundred words what would formerly have cost me ten. I can write epigrams of fifty distichs, which might be squeezed into one. I have gone the round of all my stories three or four times with the younger people, and begin them again. I give hints how significant a person I have been, and no body believes me: I pretend to pity them, but am inwardly angry. I lay traps for people to desire I would show them some things I have written, but cannot succeed; and wreak my spight, in condemning the taste of the people and company where I am. But it is with place, as it is with time. If I boast of having been valued three hundred miles off, it is of no more use than if I told how handsome I was when young.[9]

Swift may protest that he is still surrounded by a kind of rural idiocy, partly to amuse his cultured correspondent, but this picture also smiles with special irony at his own pretensions. He could always retain a self-critical talent and make it part of his writing. To live out one's life as someone who had once been esteemed, while it might be temporarily flattering, was a vain and idle refrain for a writer as intelligent and resourceful as Swift. Retirement was a pleasing fiction, but never an inspiration.

This relative lull in Swift's literary career gives us an opportunity to give proper attention to his private literary taste. What Swift read, besides what he wrote, is a less obvious but integral part of our appreciation of a life spent with literature. As if anticipating this curiosity, in August 1715 Swift wrote out a detailed, systematic inventory of his library at the Deanery.[10] He always took special care with his books, particularly when moving residence. We may recall his instructions to Rev. John Winder in 1698, when he wrote from Moor Park suggesting how his new books should be wrapped before being sent off to England. The books which he bought in England between 1710 and 1714 were packed in six boxes and followed him to his new Deanery. An inveterate list-maker, Swift in his 1715 catalogue gives us a special insight into the order of his personal life.

The catalogue reflects a meticulous sense of arrangement in his precious library, listing over six hundred titles. The books are classified both by size and character. For example, the first category is headed, 'Libri Classici Et Philogici in Folio', the second 'Libri

In Quarto' and so on, in descending order of size. Within each of these classifications, titles are arranged by genre, with the date of the edition and the price, if known, completing the entry. The sale catalogue printed after his death shows no significant increase in the extent of his library, suggesting that, in books as in opinions, he rarely extended a reliable stock. He had, however, many books given to him as gifts. To offset this increase, he lent many others which, to his great annoyance, were never returned.

Not surprisingly, more than half his library contained classical works in Greek and Latin, most of this material being philosophical and historical rather than literary, such as a heavily annotated Herodotus, and a set of thirty-one volumes on Greek and Roman antiquities, a gift from Bolingbroke. Among the few literary classics, the Greek satirist Lucian seems to have been a favourite. Swift had a habit of writing comments, in Latin, on the fly-leaf of his books, as often indicating distaste as pleasure. Remembering Temple's recommendation of the young Swift's ability with languages, it is noteworthy that over a hundred of his books were in French. Classical and contemporary history dominated his shelves, while fiction occupied the smallest section of all. He kept annotated copies of Rabelais, Cervantes, Racine and Molière, but no Shakespeare. Very little of the fiction he read was English, though he had two copies of Milton's *Paradise Lost*, and the plays of Congreve and Steele.

This is the library of a strict traditionalist (not a humourless one, however), with ambivalent interest in the contemporary literature to which he contributed so energetically. It also shows Swift's reverence for an inherited wisdom which required little improvement. Writing to Pope, several years after compiling this catalogue, he spoke of his taste in libraries: 'I hate a crowd, where I have not an easy place to see and be seen. A great library always makes me melancholy, where the best author is as much squeezed, and as obscure as a porter at a coronation.'[11] The function of a good library was to reflect a hierarchy of knowledge, to keep certain undesirable books and authors out, and to display the achievements of the past.

The pre-eminence of historical writings in the library echoes Swift's frustrated ambition to obtain the post of Historiographer Royal. Even after he accepted the Deanery, he persisted in this private obsession of explaining and justifying the role of contemporary Toryism. Given the tense political climate, it was a measure of his defiant loyalty that he would give so much of his energy to a lost cause. In early 1715, the depressing news from London prompted him to write his final essays on this laboured issue, *Memoirs, relating to that Change which happened in the Queen's Ministry in the Year 1710*, and *An Enquiry into the Behaviour of the Queen's Last Ministry*. Swift worked tirelessly at these essays over the next two years, a last, dogged effort to relieve the literary hangover from his glory-days. What is surprising about this persistence is Swift's uncharacteristically poor sense of timing. Many Tories were either no longer interested in the reputations of Oxford and Bolingbroke or, knowing more than Swift, actively discouraged fresh revelations. The *Memoirs* were finished in 1717, then laid aside, while the *Enquiry* was revised and corrected at intervals over the next twenty years. Swift was dead before his treasured histories were read by a public very different from the intended one: they were finally published in 1765 as part of his literary works. It is a sad irony that one of his most cherished literary labours should have suffered this posthumous relegation.

In these first few years at the Deanery the conventional picture of Swift as a recluse tormented by nostalgia is a bit too melodramatic to be entirely convincing. There is ample evidence, especially in the letters, that important new literary friendships developed alongside his invincible attachment to Stella, his constant friend and inspiration. In the summer of 1718, he made the acquaintance of Rev. Patrick Delany, a Junior Fellow of Trinity College Dublin, and Thomas Sheridan, a priest and schoolteacher from Cavan. These two learned and witty men remained friends of the Dean for most of his life, and joined him in several literary ventures. Delany and Sheridan's son, also called Thomas, eventually wrote two of the earliest biographies of the Dean.[12]

In October 1717, Swift and Sheridan began a playful exchange of verses on their respective characters, a poetic banter in the form of a literary duel. For Swift, who had shelved his historical researches, this was probably a most welcome opportunity to flex his wit with a man of humour and learning, in a medium he often turned to for literary relaxation. He opened the exchange with verses in Latin, 'Ad Amicum Eruditum Thomas Sheridan', a familiar version of classical eulogy displaying an intimidating command of learned allusion. Sheridan was not overwhelmed by his fatherly friend's talent for spontaneous invention, and replied in kind. Soon, however, the game turned a bit sour. The exchange of witty rebuke ended with the younger man, in reply to Swift's playful insult 'Sheridan, A Goose', resorting to what the Dean felt was unfair play. In the last quatrain of his jibe, Sheridan wrote:

> I'll write while I have half an eye in my head;
> I'll write while I live, and I'll write when you're dead.
> Tho' you call me a goose, you pitiful slave,
> I'll feed on the grass that grows on your grave.[13]

Swift was not amused. But, as befits a writer who can always transform even the slightest occasion into some imaginative design, he composed a lengthy reply to the upstart who had transgressed the boundaries of taste. He wrote the poem, 'To Mr Delany', on four sheets of paper, added an explanatory note, and posted it to the man he hoped would counsel Sheridan in poetic decorum:

> But you are to know that I have long thought severall of his Papers, and particularly that of the Funerall, to be out of all the Rules of Raillery, I ever understood, and if you think the same you ought to tell him so in the manner you like best, without bringing me into the Question, else I may be thought a Man who will not take a Jest; to avoid which Censure with you, I have sent you my thoughts on that Subject in Rime.[14]

The poem accompanying the letter is a fine exposition of Swift's simple but eloquent understanding of propriety in humour. It is part of his many writings, mostly in prose, on good breeding and cultured behaviour:

> Three Gifts for Conversation fit
> Are Humor, Raillery and Witt:
> The last, as boundless as the Wind;
> Is well conceiv'd tho not defin'd;
> For, sure, by Witt is onely meant
> Applying what we first Invent:
> What Humor is, not all the Tribe
> Of Logick-mongers can describe;
> Here, onely Nature acts her Part,
> Unhelpt by Practice, Books, or Art.
> For Wit and Humor differ quite,

> That gives Surprise, and this Delight:
> Humor is odd, grotesque, and wild,
> Onely by Affectation spoild,
> Tis never by Invention got,
> Men have it when they know it not.[15]

As a rejoinder to Sheridan's insensitivity, these lines suggested that the schoolteacher had a lot to learn from his literary master. Swift's point is that natural humour has to be civilised through the acquisition of real wit. The contemptuous reference to 'Logick-mongers' is no surprise: in matters religious, political and literary, he had no patience with philosophers. The great writer is a born writer: he reads and studies in order to polish a natural talent, not to discover it.

While Swift must have been pleased to find new friends like Delany and Sheridan, with whom he could share his sense of play and invention, he clearly wanted to stamp his authority on that friendship. After all, he was now past fifty, had once been acclaimed and feared as the greatest rhetorical talent in England, and was not going to take cheek from a Cavan cleric. Despite the misunderstanding in this early episode of Swift's new friendship, there is a striking sense of similarity with former literary escapades. His new clergyman-friends may not have been up to Windsor's cultivated standard, but Swift had soon managed to find an Irish version of literary gamesmanship. Friendships of this kind mark Swift's entire literary career, and remain the source of greatest inspiration.

The intimacy with Stella and, to a lesser extent, with Vanessa, was a similar source of inspiration, though naturally expressed in a very different form. Both women now resided in Dublin, close to the Deanery, yet we have no concrete evidence that the two objects of Swift's veneration ever met each other. In these early years at St Patrick's, he visited the women regularly, always maintaining the utmost discretion, and wrote several occasional poems for them. Although he eulogises both women in similar terms of admiration and love, it is clear from the tone of the verse for Stella that the intimacy between them was the more authentic and relaxed. In the spring of 1719, Swift wrote the first of a regular sequence of birthday poems for Stella.[16] Obviously written as a gift, these poems are touching evidence of his devotion to a woman he had first met nearly thirty years beforehand, when Swift was a young secretary at Moor Park. In 'On Stella's Birthday', the conventional praise of a woman's physical and spiritual beauty is playfully replaced by witty tribute to her intellect:

> Stella this Day is thirty-four,
> (We shan't dispute a Year or more)
> However Stella, be not troubled,
> Although thy Size and Years are doubled,
> Since first I saw thee at Sixteen
> The brightest Virgin on the Green,
> So little is thy Form declin'd
> Made up so largely in thy Mind.[17]

As far as we know, this is the first time that Swift, in his writing, refers to Esther Johnson as 'Stella'.[18] The factual inaccuracies in the opening of the poem are possibly due more to the demands of rhyme than to the poet's notorious looseness with dates. Too original and sceptical to simply play the usual role of courtly lover, Swift's praise seems authenticated by its frank concessions to time and change.

The following year he wrote two, lengthier poems celebrating her companionship and care. The first 'To Stella, Visiting me in my Sickness', is an exuberant tribute to her manly virtues, again emphasising her uniqueness as a serious, mature woman:

> Say, Stella, was Prometheus blind,
> And forming you, mistook your Kind?
> No: 'Twas for you alone he stole
> The Fire that forms a manly Soul:
> Then to compleat it ev'ry way,
> He molded it with Female Clay:
> To that you owe the nobler Flame,
> To this, the Beauty of your Frame.[19]

Stella is loved because she has none of the usual feminine vices. Her intellectual character is enhanced, not compromised, by her womanly form, a paradoxical attraction which usually provides a favourite conceit for Swift's verse about Stella. A companion-poem, 'To Stella, Who Collected and Transcribed his Poems', is a grateful tribute to her devotion, self-consciously protesting the truth behind its idealisation:

> True Poets can depress and raise;
> Are Lords of Infamy and Praise:
> They are not scurrilous in Satire,
> Nor will in Panygyrick flatter.
> Unjustly Poets we asperse;
> Truth shines the brighter, clad in Verse:
> And all the Fictions they pursue
> Do but insinuate what is true.[20]

In the comparative isolation of these years, Stella offered Swift invaluable personal, if not social, companionship and attention. The occasions for these two poems show us a very human part of that relationship in which she acted as nurse and amanuensis for a lifelong friend often marooned in the Deanery from sickness not choice.

Swift's relationship with Esther Vanhomrigh, which seemed more like a conventional, because illicit, 'affair', never inspired Swift in the same way. After the monumental 'Cadenus and Vanessa', written partly to announce the regretful but necessary termination of their London friendship, he wrote only one short poem, 'Verses to Vanessa', which he enclosed in a letter. This was in 1720, four years after she had decided to move to Ireland to be closer to him. It seems, understandably, that Swift was both flattered and alarmed by this impetuous pursuit. For most of these years, Swift tried to keep her at bay, conducting the relationship almost entirely through an emotional correspondence in which he alternated between severe warnings about propriety and untypically passionate declarations of affection and respect. He even went so far as to write a zealous letter entirely in French, blending linguistic disguise with romantic impersonation:

> . . . je ne pouvois jamais trouver aucun defaut ni en vos Actions ni en vos parolles. la Coquetrie, l'affectation, la pruderie, sont des imperfections que vous n'avois jamais connu. Et avec tout cela, croyez vous qu'il est possible de ne vous estimer au dessus du reste du genre humain. Quelles bestes en juppes sont les plus excellentes de celles que je vois semèes dans le monde au prix de vous; en les voyant, en les entendant je dis cent fois le jour – ne parle, ne regarde, ne pense, ne fait rien comme ces miserables, sont ce du meme Sexe – du meme espece de Creatures? quel cruautè de faire mepriser autant de gens qui sans songer de

vous, seroient assès supportable – Mais il est tems de vous delasser, et dire adieu avec tous le respecte, la sincerite et l'estime du monde. Je suis et seray toujours – . . .[21]

Although this effusion, written shortly before the verses commending Stella's devotion and uniqueness, rehearses the idea of a woman untypical of women, the contrast in imaginative response is self-evident. Despite the frenzied intensity of the relationship with Vanessa, it never found the same quality of response in Swift's literary heart as the bond with Stella.

Writing these occasional verses for Stella and Vanessa in his spare time, Swift reflected on romantic stereotypes of womanhood which he tried to counter through a less pompous manner and a puritanical realism. But while writing these variations on conventional love, he was inspired to write a more notorious version of female deception. This was a mocking portrait of sexual artificiality, entitled 'The Progress of Beauty', in which he details the grotesque transformation of Celia the streetwalker into an alluring Queen. Celia, first awoken, presents her real self:

> To see her from her Pillow rise
> All reeking in a cloudy Steam,
> Crack't Lips, Foul Teeth, and gummy Eyes,
> Poor Strephon, how would he blaspheme![22]

This travesty of beauty provides Swift with the desired contrast for his manly women, who are never contemplated from a physical viewpoint.[23] After a few hours at the dressing-table, Celia offers the world a foul deceit, earning the poet's brutal contempt. It is as if Swift needed to write what Ehrenpreis calls 'The Comedy of Sexual Prosthesis' to authenticate the honesty of his other romances.[24] Scatalogical realism, with its shocking contrasts of the ideal and the grotesque, is not a style which Swift reserved for women alone. Moralistic and psychoanalytic criticism have sometimes translated their own obsession into evidence of authorial neurosis. But Swift's fascination with distortion is extensive, judicial and controlled. The scatalogical pattern, setting Celia against Stella, Yahoo againt Houyhnhnm, is central to his passion for order and normality. Deficiency always angered Swift: it never made him mad.

The relative calm of Swift's first six years as Dean, I would argue,

did him an enormous amount of good as a writer. Notwithstanding
the ritualistic complaints, he discovered a new role as pastor of his
own congregation, which developed into a special kind of literary
relationship with the country itself.[25] He enjoyed a greater degree
of personal, political and literary independence than ever before.
Once the most public kind of writer imaginable, he now wrote
verse for a small group of friends, corresponded regularly and
faithfully with clerical and secular acquaintances, established a
new home of his own and, most significantly, found a ready-made
audience in his parishioners. Swift's gradual re-emergence as a
public-spirited writer owes a great deal to the discipline and
interests of his Church. After all, this was a forum in which, as a
matter of duty, he exercised his rhetorical powers of persuasion
and defence. As we shall see, this clerical role of moral guardian, in
Swift's mind inseparable from political and literary matters, shapes
and defines a later stance as witness to Ireland's tragic condition.
As early as January 1715, writing to his young friend Knightley
Chetwode, he shows a very clear awareness of his priestly duty:
'As for news, the d...l a bit do I hear, or suffer to be told me.' The
very next sentence, however, contradicts this aloofness: 'I saw in a
print that the K[ing] has taken care to limit the clergy what they
shall preach: and that has given me an inclination to preach what is
forbid: for I do not conceive there is any law yet for it.'[26] Swift was
obliged to preach at St Patrick's once every five weeks. Although
he took great care with writing and delivering his sermons, he
excluded them from publications of his work which he
supervised.[27] Such a distinction should not prevent us from seeing
the relevance of the sermons to his literary career, since Swift never
hesitated to use the pulpit for political ends. Responsible
citizenship was as much a political as a theological question.
Patrick Delany recalled Swift's sermons as no more than
'preaching pamphlets', a description attributed to the Dean himself.

On 1 December 1717, Swift preached a sermon, 'On Brotherly
Love', to his Dublin congregation. The seeming innocence of the
title completely belies the partisan interpretation. Proceeding systematically through received and current notions of Christian
charity, the preacher attacks any sympathetic application of the
idea to all men in all places, and uses the occasion to attack
Dissenters. He extracts the key-term, 'Moderation', and explains its
ambiguous and misleading use by enemies of Church and State.

Posing as an oppressed minority, Dissenters plead for toleration, but once tolerated would never tolerate others. Therefore, argues Swift, to avoid this certainty, Dissenters should not be tolerated. The word only makes sense to Swift if it has an exclusive and restricted meaning, that is toleration without power. In this passionate harangue Swift shows considerable, and alarming, skill in the selective interpretation of a language charged with political implication. Expressed in a brisk, plain style, its relentless need for fixed meaning, its abhorrence of semantic confusion, and its warning against the political corruption of language, all confirm the old Swift in renewed, fighting form.

While lecturing his audience on the evil of unlimited toleration, Swift identifies very clearly the social class of his congregation:

> The little Religion there is in the World hath been observed to reside chiefly among the middle and lower Sort of People, who are neither tempted to Pride and Luxury by great Riches, nor to desperate Courses by extreme Poverty: And truly upon that Account I have thought it a Happiness, that those who are under my immediate Care are generally of that Condition.[28]

St Patrick's position in the 'Liberties' of the city meant that a substantial part of Swift's congregation was from a class of artisans, merchants and shopkeepers, many of them in the weaving industry.[29] Out of this class emerges one of his most famous personae – the Dublin Drapier. After the years spent with the Tories in Whitehall and Windsor, his trusting identification with the 'middle and lower sort of people' is a dramatic and important development in Swift's changing loyalties. A most telling sign of this revision, one based on bitter experience, is heard in the sermon when he defines a truly moderate man as one who does not 'think it a Maxim infallible, that Virtue should always attend upon Favour, and Vice upon Disgrace'. Having written in the interests of power, he now begins to discover a much wider, and very different audience. He does not know it yet, but he is becoming the champion of honourable dissent.

In January 1720, Swift re-appeared in print for the first time in six years. This was the anonymous pamphlet, *A Letter to a Young Gentleman, Lately Enter'd into Holy Orders*, in which a well-educated and sympathetic layman offers advice to a novice clergyman on the language best suited to his public role. Having noted Swift's own care with his new, pastoral duties, it is interesting to see how ecclesiastical matters lead him back into print. He now uses his rich experience in the art of political persuasion to encourage a more forceful Church. The writer and the priest combine knowledge to produce one of Swift's most readable and eloquent lessons in artful communication.

The personalised form of this pamphlet is a well-established genre in Swift's writing. Questions of constitutionality, economy, theology and literary style are often treated in the guise of confidential advice. As far back as *The Story of the Injured Lady*, he showed his preference for dealing with abstract or difficult issues in immediate, direct and simplified form which humanised the problems. In this *Letter*, the speaker urges the intending preacher to remember his audience when sermonising: he talks as one devoted to the Church but often forced to endure tedious, inarticulate and pedantic exhibitions from the pulpit. He suggests a few guidelines for simpler, more effective communication. As a general rule, a persuasive style comes from 'Proper Words in proper Places'. He discourages obscure and slang vocabulary, learned or specialised terms, careless delivery and pronunciation and, above all, the temptation to be funny:

> I cannot forbear warning you, in the most earnest Manner, against endeavouring at Wit in your Sermons: Because, by the strictest Computation, it is very near a Million to One, that you have none; and because too many of your Calling, have consequently made themselves everlastingly ridiculous by attempting it.[30]

Wit, according to the earlier definition of style, has its proper place, but not in the dignified setting of the Church. To enhance powers of judgement and reasoning, he recommends a course of study in the classical authors, not for their questionable morality or opinions, but for their skill in expression. Finally, he appeals to the young man never to engage in theological speculation on religious mysteries: 'For, to me there seems to be a manifest Dilemma in the Case; If you explain them, they are Mysteries no longer; if you fail, you have laboured to no Purpose.'[31] Reason, in this compellingly innocent form, seems no more than commonsense. Theories do not help a God-fearing people conduct their lives in a useful manner, and are best left to 'Professors in most Arts and Sciences', who are 'generally the worst qualified to explain their Meanings to those who are not of their Tribe'. Reading one chapter of *Pilgrim's Progress*, he contends, is a better discipline than volumes of theology.

Swift uses the new social composition of his congregation to advance a crucial test of clarity for the rhetorician: '. . . a Divine hath nothing to say to the wisest Congregation of any Parish in this Kingdom, which he may not express in a Manner to be understood by the meanest among them.'[32] A plain style, 'In short, that Simplicity, without which no human Performance can arrive to any great Perfection', is defined as a social necessity. This shows, yet again, Swift's keen awareness of the public character and consequence of language. Living and working in Ireland, a country he associated with backwardness and barbarism, intensified this missionary zeal on the importance of style and decorum. Style is defined as a form of compromise between preacher and audience or writer and reader.

These views on language (to call them Swift's 'theory' would be missing his point), are deeply influenced by his cultural and political traditionalism, which regularly took its cue from the supposed decadence of contemporary civilisation. They provided the drama in *A Tale Of A Tub*, reappeared in the *Tatler*, and inspired his *Proposal* on language addressed to Oxford.[33] His conservatism, however, never quite prepares us for the originality and daring of his style. The grossest misinterpretation of Swift is to equate this conservatism with dullness. While many of his thoughts on these questions are drastic historical simplifications, his treatment of them in terms of a personal style which is flexible, direct and unpretentious, makes him a worthy humanist critic of language as a social tool. He is conservative without being a snob, a radical in search of stability.

Swift's self-image of a wounded and weary loner began to fade in the face of political events in Ireland which rekindled his old polemical spirit. At the end of 1719, he described this thaw to Ford:

> But as the World is now turned, no Cloyster is retired enough to keep Politicks out, and I will own they raise my Passions whenever they come in my way, perhaps more than yours who live amongst them, as a great noise is likelyer to disturb a Hermit than a Citizen.[34]

Two major legal pronouncements from London gradually provoked Swift into action. The first of these was what became known
as the Annesley Case.[35] This began as an internal legal dispute over
property rights, and was finally settled by a declaration from
London that the Irish House of Lords had no appellate jurisdiction.
In March 1720, this rebuke to the authority of the Irish parliament
was solemnised in a Declaratory Act 'for the better securing the
Dependency of Ireland'. These related pieces of political legislation, which confirmed the worst suspicions of Irish Protestants,
became and remained a fundamental point of reference for everything Swift wrote about Ireland. We should also remember that, in
Swift's eyes, the present Whig administration had usurped the
place of his closest political friends. He might feign indifference,
but he had an unforgiving memory. Treating Ireland with contempt was not the only evidence of Whig perfidy: part of Swift's
motivation was a readiness and ability to settle a long-standing
account with these champions of so-called 'Toleration'.

A month after the Declaratory Act was published, Swift wrote
again to Ford, this time strongly airing his views on such discriminatory law:

> ... the Question is whether People ought to be Slaves or no. It is
> like the Quarrel against Convocations; they meet but seldom,
> have no Power, and for want of those Advantages, cannot make
> any Figure when they are suffered to assemble. You fetter a Man
> seven years, then let him loose to shew his Skill in dancing, and
> because he does it awkwardly, you say he ought to be fetterd for
> Life.[36]

The contradictions of Anglo-Irish relations brought out some of
Swift's most entertaining and ingenious ironies. Free from political
control and patronage, he could now take up a classic stand
against the tyranny of power. In this case, power lay, conveniently,
in the hands of a party he already associated with corruption. It
should be stressed, however, that when Swift first began to
champion Ireland's rights, he did so alongside widespread official
and popular protest. He never instigated trouble: but he was
always the protest's most daring and eloquent supporter.[37]

At the end of May 1720, Swift published his first pamphlet on
Irish affairs since becoming Dean. Entitled *A Proposal for the
Universal Use of Irish Manufacture*, it is an angry dismissal of Eng-

land's colonial treatment of Ireland's economy and, by way of retaliation, an appeal for a national boycott of English trade. Although its subject is political economy, its style is colloquial and sardonic:

> I heard the late Archbishop of Tuam mention a pleasant Observation of some Body's; *that Ireland would never be happy 'till a Law were made for burning every Thing that came from England, except their People and their Coals*: I must confess, that as to the former, I should not be sorry if they would stay at home; and for the latter, I hope, in a little Time we shall have no Occasion for them.[38]

The tone becomes increasingly provocative and derisory, paying sarcastic compliments to landlords who have ruined the economy, sympathising with English bishops who claim poverty, mimicking those who have an irrational preference for English over Irish products, and pointing out women as prime agents of careless and unpatriotic economy. With grim patience, he politely enquires whether 'a Law to bind Men without their own Consent, be obligatory *in foro Conscientiae*', since neither Scripture nor Reason offer any help in this matter. Some rhetorical flourishes employ a Biblical authority for their paradoxical reflections:

> The Scripture tells us, that *Oppression makes a wise Man mad*, therefore, consequently speaking, the Reason why some Men are not *mad*, is because they are not *wise*: However, it were to be wished that *Oppression* would, in time, teach a little *Wisdom* to Fools.[39]

Speaking from his literary pulpit, Swift finds the language of riddles quite appropriate to a situation which defies reason and offends common sense. After six years of reserve, his first polemic on Ireland is like an eruption of impatience and scorn, marked by some evidence of his old talents, but overall lacking a coherent design.

Nobody, especially Swift, expected the legal drama which the pamphlet created. Although it was timed to appear just before the King's birthday, on 28 May, it seemed to avoid constitutional defiance in favour of internal criticism. In any event, on 30 May the Grand Juries of Dublin City and County proclaimed the pamphlet as 'false, scandalous, and seditious'. For the second time in his

literary career, but not for the last time in Ireland, Swift's writing
was up against the law. The printer, Edmund Waters, in the
absence of a named author, was immediately arrested and sent for
trial before the Chief Justice Whitshed. An obstinate jury, repeatedly sent back by Whitshed when it continued to find in the printer's
favour, finally returned a special verdict which obliged the zealous
Judge to decide for himself. He deferred the case, and Waters
remained in prison. Swift then began a discreet campaign to free
the unfortunate printer. Five months later, in October, he wrote to
Sir Thomas Hanmer, Speaker of the English House of Commons,
asking him to use his influence. Swift dismissed the fuss over the
pamphlet as wholly disproportionate to what he called 'a weak
hasty Scribble', saying there was nothing in the work 'of Whig or
Tory reflecting upon any Person whatsoever'. Whitshed's desire to
make a name for himself was, suggested Swift, the real cause of the
controversy. He specifically asked Hanmer to approach the incom-
ing Lord Lieutenant of Ireland, the Duke of Grafton, and propose a
pardon. In August 1721, over a year after the pamphlet had first
appeared, Grafton used his power to quash the case with the grant
of a *noli prosequi* judgement.

The political pattern of this drama seemed ominous, and was to
be repeated many times in Swift's writings on Ireland. It showed
Swift that the government took special exception to protest from
Irish Protestants, and was unreasonably sensitive to their complaints. Swift was hardly a novice in the laws affecting political
pamphlets. Instinctively, he had gone straight to the top of the
government, as he had done in England, to present his version of
the case and remind people of his familiarity with channels of
influence. Most significantly, Protestant Ireland saw that it had a
new voice, experienced, resolute and sympathetic. At the age of
fifty-three, Swift had begun a new career as a radical writer.

Retirement invigorated rather than diminished his imagination.
England always remained a crucial, unavoidable touchstone for his
ideas and values, but he had developed a more ambivalent,
shrewder perspective on her political behaviour. His most definitive reassessment is the *Letter to Mr Pope*, written in January 1721, a
year after the *Proposal*, in which he reaffirms his political consistency. More immediately, he defends his integrity as a writer abused
and threatened by tyrannical laws.[40]

Using his favourite epistolary form of address, the 'letter' is a
personalised essay in which he patiently and systematically de-

fines his principles as citizen and writer. He begins by explaining his earlier silence as a way of life 'not taken up out of any sort of Affectation, but merely to avoid giving offence, and for fear of provoking Party-zeal'. He deals contemptuously with the provocation which a writer in Ireland must endure. Openly pointing to the Whitshed case against his *Proposal*, he reflects derisively on the danger of being a writer with opinions:

> For however orthodox they may be while I am now writing, they may become criminal enough to bring me into trouble before midsummer. And indeed I have often wished for some time past, that a political Catechism might be published by authority four times a year, in order to instruct us how we are to speak and write, and act during the current quarter.[41]

As never before, Swift now defends the rights and responsibilities of a public-spirited writer threatened by censorship and legal bullying. Angry at such wilful misinterpretation of his work, indignant at being represented as the author of all anonymous, subversive pamphlets, he concludes with a calmly self-critical profile of his literary power:

> For, however I may have been sowered by personal ill-treatment, or by melancholy prospects for the publick, I am too much a politician to expose my own safety by offensive words: and, if my genius and spirit be sunk by encreasing years, I have at least enough discretion left, not to mistake the measure of my own abilities, by attempting subjects where those talents are necessary, which perhaps I may have lost with my youth.[42]

Swift hated being taken for a fool or a second-rate scribbler. For the first time in his literary career, he realises that the writer on Irish affairs is in a most vulnerable position, but, with a conscience and a tactical sense, the writer can remind his people of their rights and liberties.

Swift's pamphlets and tracts on Ireland began, and stayed, with practical and material questions of survival. Whatever political idealism we may confer on him, economy is the dominant theme. For someone who asserted that 'Happiness is nine parts Wealth, and one part Health', this attention to the material foundation of life is to be expected. Residence and observation in Ireland confirmed this sceptical realism. Economy seems an unpromising subject for such a literary talent as Swift's, yet, as Ehrenpreis shrewdly observes, 'Money was always a key that unlocked his imagination'.[43] With his usual playful invention, Swift found many fictional designs for this subject and, most ingeniously, was able to relate them to the satirical fantasies of his early writing. In the last paragraph of the 1720 *Proposal*, in the style of an afterthought, Swift notes 'a Thing, they call a Bank, which, I hear, is projecting in this Town'. In the summer of that year, the King had formally approved a project to establish a national bank for Ireland. Unfortunately for its backers, but conveniently for Swift, the scheme was tainted by association with the spectacular collapse of the South Sea Bubble earlier that year.[44] Thousands of speculators had lost fortunes in that exotic investment. For Swift, such adventurism, if transferred to Ireland and institutionalised, would rob the country of its remaining senses as well as cash. His understanding of this financial enterprise, however eccentric it may seem to us, is easily related to his impatience with all kinds of speculation. Intelligent but anti-intellectual, he argued that a bank would serve private, not public, interests, that paper money and credit would only further impoverish a shaky economy.

Joining in the public debate at the end of 1720, he published a series of short lampoons and broadsides on the folly of the scheme.[45] Several of these comic sketches parody the advertisements for freak-shows and circus-entertainments in which spectacular and incredible feats are promised. The language of these appeals is suitably exaggerated, such as the title *The Wonder of All the Wonders that Ever the World Wondered At*, and the lurid account which follows describes a catalogue of outrageous performances, such as the following:

> He lets any Gentleman drink a Quart of hot melted Lead; and by a Draught of prepared Liquor, of which he takes part himself, he makes the said Lead pass through the said Gentleman before all the Spectators, without any Damage: After which it is produced in a Cake to the Company.[46]

The imagination behind this, which develops a conceit between speculation and bodily functions, derives from *A Tale Of A Tub*, in which those other charlatans, the free-thinkers and dissenters, were reduced to figures of noisome wind. The financial projector is a species of lunatic whose preposterous vision can only be compared to the irrational hold of Popery over the intelligence of its subscribers. In another squib, *The Swearer's Bank*, Swift outlines an alternative mock-proposal whereby the widespread habit of cursing, if taxed and then collected, could be turned into a national asset. The most effective of these Bank papers, it is generally agreed, is *A Letter from a Lady*, in which a woman, tempted to deposit her entire savings with this chimerical institution, is rescued at the last minute by her friend's direct observation of the deceit. It is typical of Swift to select a woman to represent the gullibility which such desperate schemes exploit. Her close shave with financial ruin is told in a patient and heartfelt style, giving the piece a credible persona. Like the *Story of the Injured Lady*, it is based on a convention of traditional gallantry which makes the present scheme seem typical of modern dishonour. By a satisfying coincidence, the *Letter* appeared on the very day that the Irish Houses defeated a bill to introduce the bank, perhaps a small sign to Swift of the efficacy of such involvement.

Swift's pessimism was temporarily disappointed by this success. He wrote to Chetwode:

> You hear the bank was kicked out with ignominy last Saturday. This subject filled the town with pamphlets ... As to my own part, I mind little what is doing out of my proper dominions, the Liberties of the Deanery; yet I thought a bank ought to be established and would be so because it was the only ruinous thing wanting to the kingdom, and therefore I had not the least doubt but that the Parliament would pass it.[47]

In his 'proper dominions' around the deanery, Swift showed his practical concern for the weavers by publicising their economic condition as often as possible. Their industry had been badly affected by English legislation, with widespread unemployment and poverty much in evidence. Fundraising activities for distressed families included a special performance of *Hamlet* at the Theatre Royal on 11 April 1721, for which Sheridan wrote a special prologue and Swift an epilogue. These verses were recited on stage by individual actors. Both pieces encouraged the captive audience to set an example by wearing only Irish cloth and wool. Swift's epilogue tried to blend the local and the mythical to suit the occasion:

> We'll Rig in Meath-Street, Egypt's hauty Queen,
> And Anthony shall court her in Ratteen.
> In blew shalloon, shall Hanniball be Clad,
> And Scipio, trail an Irish purple Plad.[48]

The verse does its best with several tortured analogies, but the benefit raised seventy-three pounds, and Swift had done his duty. Together with Sheridan's prologue, Swift's contribution was printed by John Harding as a memorial sheet. Harding had earlier printed some of the Dean's Bank pamphlets: in a few years time he would be entrusted with *The Drapier's Letters*.

Swift was beginning to discover Ireland. Indifference was never part of his literary personality: it should be viewed, rather, as a literary screen behind which he rested his energies. He enjoyed the love and devotion of Stella, the literary companionship of a small circle of friends, new contacts in the publishing world, and the satisfaction of writing about public affairs without political supervision. There is even some evidence that he ventured into the literary culture of the Gaelic majority. It is worth remembering that Dublin, as the centre of government and administration, was almost entirely an English-speaking city, in which it was easy to ignore or forget the presence of the 'other' nation, several millions of people with a language and culture utterly different from Swift's.[49] Clergymen like himself lived on anglicised islands in a sea of alienated, Gaelic-speaking Catholics. Dublin, however, contained many literary and scholarly figures, not all of them in the English tradition. It is certain that Swift was aware of a second literary culture alongside his own. In 1720, he wrote a lively version of a comic Gaelic poem, *Pléaraca na Ruarcach*, which he re-titled 'The Description of an Irish Feast'. While staying with the Sheridan family in Quilca, County Cavan, Swift had been supplied with a literal translation by the author himself, Hugh MacGauran. Delighted with the humorous and rhythmic possibilities of the original, which described an uproarious country feast of extravagant proportions, Swift composed a rollicking version in his own style:

> O'Rourk's noble Fare
> Will ne'er be forgot,
> By those who were there,
> Or those who were not.

His Revels to keep,
We sup and we dine,
On seven Score Sheep,
Fat Bullocks and Swine.
Usquebagh to our Feast
In Pails was brought up,
A Hundred at least,
And a Madder our Cup.[50]

In this sporting verse there is something of Swift's old love for vivid, enumerative detail and bathetic humour, aspects refined in his 'Description' poems of London, written a decade beforehand. His version of the translation also shows us something about Swift's travels in Ireland, and his detailed familiarity with place and province. The original Gaelic uses the names of towns in the west such as Boyle, Sligo and Galway: Swift changes them to reflect his own side of the country, substituting Lusk, Slane and Kildare, places he frequently travelled through on journeys between Dublin and Laracor.

Despite his age and ill health, Swift undertook some extraordinarily arduous journeys around Ireland. In the early summer of 1722, he rode north to visit friends in Tyrone, Armagh and Cavan. While staying with the Cope family in Loughgall, just outside the ecclesiastical city of Armagh, he wrote to Vanessa, telling her of the terrible scenes of poverty and misery he had witnessed every day of his journey. Once arrived, his only consolation was that in Protestant Loughgall, 'the People, the Churches and the Plantations make me think I am in England'. He spent most of his time reading 'diverting Books of History and Travells', later dismissing them as 'abundance of Trash'.

We know that Swift had already written sections of *Gulliver's Travels*, for in April of the previous year he had written to Ford: 'I am now writing a History of my Travells, which will be a large Volume, and gives Account of Countryes hitherto unknown; but they go on slowly for want of Health and Humor.'[51] While staying in Loughgall, Swift received a letter from Vanessa which described her disgust with people at a recent social gathering:

... they were so very Obsequious their form's and gestures were very like those of Babboons and monky's they all grin'd and chatter'd at the same time and that of things I did not under-

stand ... one of these animals snatched my fan and was so
pleased with me that it seased me with such a panick that I
apprehended nothing less than being carried up to the top of the
House and served as a friend of yours was ...[52]

Harold Williams suggests, quite convincingly, that Vanessa had
been shown part of the *Travels* by Swift, and that here she is
alluding to Chapter Five of the voyage to Brobdingnag. There is
something of the Trojan horse about Swift's career during these
months, lamenting everything about Ireland while exploring it,
regretting his literary decline while secretively composing his
magnum opus. A tantalising harmony between biography and
imagination also offers itself in the prospect of Swift, like Gulliver,
engaged in a series of expeditions through strange, barbarous
landscapes. Is it too much to suggest that, once he conceived the
fiction of his *Travels*, these long, solitary journeys across Ireland
stimulated the possibilities of that fiction?[53] In his 1720 *Proposal*, he
had already characterised the country as somewhere utterly
beyond civilisation: 'Whoever travels this Country, and observes
the *Face* of Nature, or the *Faces*, and Habits, and Dwellings of the
Natives, will hardly think himself in a Land where either *Law*,
Religion, or common Humanity is professed.'[54] The fantastical imagery of *Gulliver's Travels* and, of course, *A Modest Proposal*, is already
taking shape.

The correspondence between Swift and Vanessa reached a crisis
in that summer of 1722, after which no letters survive. She became
increasingly impatient with Swift's prolonged absences and excuses, and he seems to have closed their relationship for the
second time. Vanessa died, at the age of thirty-three, in June
1723.[55] To avoid any hint of scandal, Swift set off again, immediately after her funeral, on yet another journey. He rode as far south as
the rugged coastline of West Cork, over two hundred miles from
Dublin. At a place called Carbery, he was so enthralled by the wild
sublimity of the landscape that he composed a romantic apos-
trophe to the scene, 'Carberiae Rupes', a classical tribute entirely in
Latin.[56] He was always pleased with his poetic exercises in the
classical tongue, and took special care to see it was eventually
printed along with his English verse. After Cork, he turned west
to County Galway, where he stayed with Bishop Bolton in Clon-
fert. He wrote to Sheridan that he was 'half weary with the four
hundred miles I have rode', but added that he would try to get

back to Dublin for the opening of Parliament, by the Duke of Grafton, at the end of the month.

These rambles had lasted just over two months. Within a year, he had ridden through the four provinces of Ireland, storing images and observations which he would put to powerful use in controversies to come. After nearly ten years of continual residence, he could now speak with the authority of experience in England as well as a renewed intimacy with Ireland. There is something impressive in the picture of this middle-aged Dean, once a favourite of the court at Windsor, travelling alone through the wilds of the Irish landscape, his imagination full of Gulliver's exotic voyages, finally turning back towards Dublin to face the most celebrated years of his literary career.

5

Literary Triumph in Ireland and England

During Swift's rambles in the summer of 1723, an economic controversy had emerged in Dublin which was soon to engage him as a supreme pamphleteer in the guise of a Dublin Drapier. This was the issue of Wood's halfpence, which began as a legislative dispute between Dublin and London over money, and ended with Swift asserting Ireland's right to legislative independence, while exposing the injustice and corruption of the English administration.

This extraordinary episode in Swift's literary career began without his knowledge or involvement.[1] In July 1722, while the Dean was drafting *Gulliver's Travels*, William Wood, a financial speculator from Wolverhampton, had managed to secure a patent for coining money for the Irish economy. Protests from official circles in Dublin, including Archbishop King and the Commissioners of Revenue, pointed out that such an important decision had been taken without any consultation in Ireland, where the project was viewed as both insensitive and unnecessary. Swift first mentions this dangerous distraction in a letter to Ford, nearly two years after the patent was originally granted, when he was trying to finish *Gulliver's Travels*.[2]

It seems likely that Swift was willingly encouraged by friends to write something for the established opposition to the patent.[3] As he himself later remarked, he was both welcomed and provoked into this argument. By the spring of 1724, he had joined a well-defined, respectable body of official resistance to this arbitrary imposition: his rhetorical contribution, humanised through the pseudonymous mask of a humble but determined shopkeeper, would popularise the Irish case in dramatic and effective fashion. Suspending work on his satire, he now saw an opportunity to stand forward as spokesman for his own countrymen and teach them a lesson in liberty.

Masquerading as an ordinary, concerned citizen, over the next eighteen months Swift wrote seven pamphlets on the controversy. These were *A Letter to the Shopkeepers*, *A Letter to Mr Harding*, *Some Observations upon a Paper, called The Report*, *A Letter to the Whole People of Ireland*, *A Letter to Lord Viscount Molesworth*, *A Letter to Lord Chancellor Middleton*, and *A Humble Address to Both Houses of Parliament*. The last two pamphlets in this sequence were not published until 1735, for legal and tactical reasons. The first pamphlet, *To the Shopkeepers*, appeared in March and established the fiction of the persona for the entire campaign, 'no inconsiderable Shop-keeper in this Town', a plain-spoken citizen duty-bound to alert his countrymen to impending disaster. His argument, expressed in a direct, confident, well-researched style, is that no law exists which compels people to accept bad coinage, especially when there is no consultation. Speaking as if this pamphlet was the end of his contribution, Swift wrote to Ford:

> I do not know whether I told you that I sent out a small Pamphlet under the Name of a Draper, laying the whole Vilany open, and advising People what to do; about 2000 of them have been dispersed by Gentlemen in severall Parts of the Country, but one can promise nothing from such Wretches as the Irish people.[4]

Swift's characteristic pessimism is less remarkable than the large number of copies printed and the personalised scheme of distribution. Relishing precision in matters of money and class, the Drapier begins by addressing his peers, while his text is circulated by 'Gentlemen'. If 'national' opposition was to mean anything, Swift knew that his Drapier would have to appeal to several classes. The titular pattern of *The Drapier's Letters* shows a systematic appeal to a hierarchical set of economic groups, united by national and self-interest. Well into the Drapier's campaign, he delighted in the paradoxical and unforeseen unity achieved: '*Money*, the great *Divider* of the World, hath, by a strange Revolution, been the great *Uniter* of a most *divided* People.'[5] The Drapier's crusade, by uniting the Protestant interest in Ireland, created a version of 'national' consensus which was always Swift's deepest political desire.

Alarmed by the determined opposition in Ireland, London replaced the ineffectual Duke of Grafton with a new Lord Lieutenant, Cartaret. As it turned out, this was to Swift's advantage, since they were old friends from the days of Queen Anne's court. Quick to remind Cartaret of their former closeness, Swift wrote a congra-

tulatory letter, expressing his hope that the patent would be
withdrawn by such an enlightened governor. Maintaining his
dignified but cordial manner, Swift enclosed a copy of *To the
Shopkeepers*, remarking with daring nonchalance that it 'is entitled
to a Weaver, and suited to the vulgar, but thought to be the work of
a better hand'.[6] There is little doubt that Cartaret knew the identity
of the Drapier, but these two friends were now representing
opposed interests: each was determined to do his job.[7]

Swift's printer, John Harding, played a crucial role in the
Drapier's campaign. Harding was both an adventurous printer and
the owner of the Dublin *Weekly News-Letter*, an outlet which Swift
used regularly for advertising aspects of the Drapier's case. On 6
August 1724, the second pamphlet, *To Mr Harding*, appeared. After
waiting several months for a fresh target, the Drapier now re-
sponded to a report in Harding's newspaper which quoted Wood's
contempt for the Irish opposition. Written to remind Harding and,
through him, printers and newspaper-owners in general, of their
civic responsibility to publish the truth in matters concerning the
public welfare, the Drapier castigates Wood, 'this little Arbitrary
Mock-Monarch', for daring to set his private interest against that of
a loyal nation. The Drapier's real concern is that the Irish people,
like those who subscribed to the South Sea Bubble, will be
hypnotised by this arrogant speculator, 'therefore, I confess, it is
my chief Endeavour to keep up your Spirits and Resentments.'
Like a watchman at the gates of Sion, the Drapier now writes as
guardian and defender of a besieged people. On 25 August, the
third pamphlet, *Some Observations*, developed this stand. This was
the Drapier's considered and systematic reply to the official report
by the English Privy Council on Wood's scheme. The Council, to
the surprise of nobody in Ireland, had endorsed the project. Since
the enquiry had only heard English witnesses, arbitrary rule
without consent seemed now a tactic as well as a principle. The
Drapier's reply, subtitled, 'To the Nobility and Gentry of the
Kingdom of Ireland', points out to the Irish ruling class the
enormity of such a snub. By now, the issues had developed from
the economic to the political, from the personal to the national.
Straining to enlighten and alert his superiors, and 'Having already
written Two Letters to People of my own Level and Condition', the
Drapier declares his strategy for dealing with legal and constitutional jargon: 'How shall I, a poor ignorant Shop-keeper, utterly

unskilled in Law, be able to answer so weighty an Objection? I will try what can be done by plain Reason, unassisted by Art, Cunning, or Eloquence.'[8] The Drapier's popularity and credibility come from his class and style. Being a trader, he deals with real, not invisible, money; as an intelligent but unsophisticated man, he is perfectly placed to demand simple and practical definitions from a legal system which uses language to mystify and subordinate people.

By the summer of 1724, scores of solemn declarations were drawn up by official bodies, corporations, guilds, even the Grand Jury of County Dublin, all swearing to boycott Wood's halfpence. This tactic, first urged by Swift in his 1720 *Proposal for the Universal Use of Irish Manufacture*, had become central to the Drapier's strategy. It must have seemed to Cartaret, who was due in Dublin at the end of October, that his old friend, a master of political disguise and literary opportunism, had effectively inspired the nation to challenge English rule in Ireland. Swift now wrote a fourth pamphlet to coincide with the Lord Lieutenant's arrival on 22 October, a calculated challenge to his Majesty's representative. Grandly but simply entitled, *To the Whole People of Ireland*, this most provocative of the *Letters* created an immediate legal sensation, and confirmed the Drapier as Ireland's patriotic hero.

Aware of the limits of sectional pleading, Swift wisely confronted the authorities with a pamphlet which claimed, with good but limited reason, to speak for all interests in Ireland. This pamphlet rises above the technical and personal issues of the previous pamphlets, and conducts itself with a rhetorical authority and a stylistic confidence suitable to the gravity and outrageousness of the issue involved. The Drapier makes it clear that it is now a question of Ireland's constitutional status and integrity. This allows him to examine the whole system whereby England exploits Ireland, a system which allows people like Wood to rob an entire country for personal gain. In blatantly deferential references to Cartaret, he assures his audience that such corruption will have no place under the new administration. Some of the Drapier's most daring and aggressive rhetoric is heard in this pamphlet, as when he reaches a climax of indignation and resolution:

> The Remedy is wholly in your own Hands; and therefore I have digressed a little, in order to refresh and continue that *Spirit* so seasonably raised among you; and to let you see, that by the

Laws of GOD, of NATURE, of NATIONS, and of your own Country, you ARE and OUGHT to be as FREE a People as your Brethren in *England*.[9]

Sometimes this crude typographical emphasis gives way to witty and shocking imagery, but the message remains the same:

For in *Reason*, all *Government* without the Consent of the *Governed*, is the *very Definition of Slavery*: But in *Fact*, *Eleven Men well armed*, *will certainly subdue one single Man in his Shirt*. But I have done. For those who have used *Power* to cramp *Liberty*, have gone so far as to resent even the *Liberty of Complaining*; although a Man upon the Rack, was never known to be refused the Liberty of *roaring* as loud as he thought fit.[10]

However grotesque Ireland's position, the Drapier felt there was nothing disrespectful, let alone subversive, in this kind of complaint. Swift knew better, which is precisely why he chose a relatively innocent persona to proclaim the outrage, someone who had not lost a basic idealism by which the present corruption could be exposed as unnatural and repugnant.

On 27 October, exactly a week after the pamphlet appeared, Cartaret summoned the Irish Privy Council, which issued a proclamation against the pamphlet on the grounds of sedition, and offered a reward of three hundred pounds to anyone who would reveal the author.[11] For the second time in four years, the Dean of St Patrick's was the prime suspect for what the authorities considered an illegal publication. In the next four weeks, there ensued an extraordinary legal intrigue, not without its comic moments. Popular support for the Drapier stood firm, and a Scriptural verse appeared overnight in many public places around Dublin:

And the people said unto Saul, Shall Jonathan die, who hath wrought this great salvation in Israel? God forbid: as the Lord liveth, there shall not one hair of his head fall to the ground, for he hath wrought with God this day. So the people rescued Jonathan, and he died not.[12]

Given Swift's fictional gamesmanship, it is not unlikely that he arranged this Biblical support himself. But on 7 November, the printer Harding and his wife were arrested. Brought before a grand jury, presided over by Chief Justice Whitshed (who conducted the prosecution against Swift's 1720 *Proposal*), Harding declared his innocence of seditious intent and his ignorance of the author's identity. In a crafty (and illegal) move, Swift wrote an anonymous broadside called *Seasonable Advice*, addressed to the jury members, and had it printed immediately. In it he warned the jury not to be bullied, and reminded them that the issue was Wood not Harding, patriotism not sedition. Faced with such a scandalous intervention, the judge instructed the jury to proclaim against the broadside instead of the original pamphlet. The jury declined and was dismissed by a frustrated and humiliated Whitshed. Like some ghostly tormentor, Swift hit back at the judge yet again. He discovered a precedent from 1680 proving the illegality of Whitshed's behaviour, and had it printed and distributed throughout Dublin. Finally, on 28 November, a month after the original proclamation, the second jury issued a 'Presentment' to Whitshed. Ignoring the issues of sedition and influencing a jury, it repeated the legality of resistance to the patent, and paid tribute to 'all such Patriots, as have been eminently zealous for the Interest of his Majesty, and this Country, in detecting the fraudulent Imposition of the said Wood'. The entire statement, unknown to the seething judge, was written by Swift!

During this legal farce, Swift had been finishing another pamphlet, *To Middleton*, the Lord Chancellor in Ireland.[13] This was the only pamphlet in the *Letters* which Swift signed in his own name, deciding it was now safe enough to publish his support for the Drapier, without admitting they were one and the same person. He quickly changed his mind when he saw how serious Cartaret felt about pursuing the author. This personalised pamphlet to one of the most powerful men in the Irish establishment (who had voted to prosecute the 1720 *Proposal* and, only days before Swift wrote to him, signed the proclamation against the fourth pamphlet) is written in a serious and calm manner, addressing Middleton as an equal in understanding and loyalty. Swift knew that Middleton was opposed to Wood, but behind the prosecution. Respectfully but forcefully, he insists on the legitimacy of the Irish protest by reminding the Chancellor of the grave and fundamental liberties involved. These include the freedom of the press. As so often in these *Letters*, he uses the English practice (and his own experience) as a critical contrast to the Irish situation in order to expose and reject double standards: 'When a bill is debating in either House of Parliament there, nothing is more usual, than to have the Controversy handled by Pamphlets on both Sides; without the least Animadversion upon the Authors.'[14] While he was working for the Tories, such tolerance was a threat to Swift: now it was a principled necessity. Ireland usually makes Swift sound more liberal on issues like this. Although he withheld publication of the pamphlet to Middleton, the intention was consistent with the strategy of the *Letters*. By singling out the representative of the Irish legal system, Swift hoped to extend the respectability and urgency of the Drapier's earlier arguments.

The fifth, and last, of the *Letters* to be published during the crisis, was *To Molesworth*, signed by the Drapier not Swift, which appeared on 31 December. This is the most playful and spirited of the series. Although the patent had still not been withdrawn, the grand juries had defied the legislature, Cartaret had been sidetracked from the issue of sedition, popular support was as strong as ever, and Swift had been protected from arrest by a sympathetic public of all ranks. As in the previous, unpublished pamphlet, he aimed at another distinguished individual amongst the ruling class, but one more sympathetic to the patriotic Drapier. Viscount Molesworth was a former Privy Counsellor, a radical Whig noted for his hostility to the Declaratory Act which had defined Ireland as a 'depending Kingdom'. The letter to him says little new about Wood, since that aspect is largely exhausted. Instead, it explores the principles and necessity of patriotism during such a constitutional threat. In an elaborate allegorical use of the Drapier's autobiography, Swift comes tantalisingly close to revealing himself as the voice behind the figurehead of the shopkeeper. Alluding to his earlier work for the Tories, but preserving the fiction of an eloquent trader, he pretends to a sense of shock and disillusionment on returning to Ireland:

> . . . this Habit of Writing and Discoursing, wherein I unfortunately differ from *almost* the whole Kingdom, and am apt to grate the Ears of more than I could wish; was acquired during my apprenticeship in *London*, and a long Residence there after I had set up for my self. Upon my Return and Settlement here, I thought I had only *changed one Country of Freedom for another*.[15]

Speaking indirectly through an ingénu like the Drapier was Swift's most effective way of raising fundamental principles with honest conviction but without the distraction of any obvious political sectarianism. Idealistic and innocent adherence to the principle of equality becomes the distinctive irony in this pamphlet. Genuinely amazed by the fuss over his writings, the Drapier confesses to Molesworth 'that the boldest and most obnoxious Words I ever delivered, would in England have only exposed me as a stupid Fool, who went to prove that the Sun shone in a clear Summer's Day'. The most extraordinary aspect of this ironic pleading is that it could be devised by a writer who had already experienced deep cynicism and yet could assert, with passion and conviction, the original principles such cynicism had displaced.

By the New Year, both sides in the dispute were waiting to see what would happen: the government hoping that opposition would fade through fatigue, the Drapier's supporters confident the patent would be withdrawn. Parliament was prorogued until August. In April, to keep the patriotic spirit alive during this lull, and as a public gesture of solidarity, Dublin councillors conferred the freedom of the city upon the Dean of St Patrick's. A grateful but evasive Swift then left for Quilca, Co. Cavan, to stay with the family of his friend Sheridan. Here he intended to rest and finish his work on *Gulliver's Travels*. By May, the six-month limit for claiming the reward for identifying the author of *Seasonable Advice* had elapsed, which gave Swift some sense of advantage. Knowing that the Irish parliament was to open in August, he started writing the seventh and final letter on the patent, signed by the Drapier. Having begun with his own class, the Drapier had moved up through the social hierarchy, and now concluded with a direct appeal to the seat of Irish authority.

The *Humble Address* is quite different from the previous pamphlets. The fiction of the Drapier is far less in evidence, providing a very flimsy cover for Swift's programme of economic reforms which he entrusts to the Irish parliament. Anyone familiar with his 1720 *Proposal* will see that this seminal pamphlet is once again revived and elaborated. Self-reliance, boycott of unnecessary imports, encouragement of tillage and afforestation, elimination of absenteeism – these are what the Drapier calls 'modest Proposals' offered, not as advice, but as 'the Nation's Wishes'. Refusing to act the sceptic, Swift makes the Drapier sound as solemn and formal as possible, reminding the parliament of its divine authority:

... whenever You shall please to impose *Silence* upon me, I will submit; because, I look upon your *unanimous Voice* to be the *Voice* of the Nation; and this I have been taught, and do believe to be, in some Manner, the *Voice of God*.[16]

Swift's syntactical emphasis makes it clear that only the Irish, and never the English, parliament commands his allegiance. Since he had, in fact, little regard for the Irish assembly, we can interpret this as a calculated ultimatum to a parliament which should learn to behave with self-respect.

Biding his time in Quilca, Swift sent off the *Humble Address* to friends in Dublin, with clear instructions that it should appear the day on which the new parliament opened. But Cartaret postponed the opening, and Swift's friends began to alter the manuscript, taking upon themselves the role of legal censor. At the end of August, vexed and frustrated, Swift wrote to his friend, Rev. John Worrall, 'I gave Jack Grattan the papers corrected, and, I think half spoiled, by the cowardly caution of him and others.' They had, he felt, misinterpreted prudence as fear. He did not know that on the previous day to this letter, on 26 August, the Irish Privy Council had formally announced the revocation of Wood's patent. On receiving the news, a week later, Swift wrote back to Worrall:

> Since Wood's patent is cancelled, it will by no means be convenient to have the paper printed, as I suppose you, and Jack Grattan, and Sheridan will agree; therefore, if it be with the printer, I would have it taken back, and the press broke, and let her be satisfied. The work is done, and there is no more need of the Drapier.[17]

The language makes clear Swift's pragmatic attitude towards such writing. Once the occasion is removed, such pamphlets are unnecessary. Commercial printers and publishers, eager to capitalise on Swift's reputation, did not accept such workmanlike distinctions.

Through the mask of the Drapier, Swift came to define a new role for himself as a writer, one as protector and guardian of the public interest. His profession, political situation, and literary instinct combined to create a rhetorical stance as patriotic defender of his 'nation'. This was a heroic guise, noted in the Drapier's initials, 'M.B.', alluding to Marcus Brutus, one of Swift's most cherished figures of ancient virtue, who risked everything in the fight against corruption and tyranny.[18] Throughout the *Letters*, the Drapier's resistance is graphically and dramatically compared with figures of unlikely but courageous defiance. Many of these analogies are Biblical, as in *Some Observations*:

> I was in the Case of *David, who could not move in the Armour of Saul*; and therefore I rather chose to attack this *uncircumcised Philistine* (*Wood* I mean) *with a Sling and a Stone*. And I may say for *Wood*'s Honour, as well as my own, that he resembles *Goliath* in many Circumstances, very applicable to the present Purpose.[19]

Swift also drew on his classical learning to deliver instructive and edifying warning, as with the fable from Demosthenes in *Seasonable Advice*:

> Once upon a Time, the *Wolves* desired a League with the *Sheep*, upon this Condition: That the Cause of Strife might be taken away, which was the *Shepherds* and *Mastiffs*: This being granted, the *Wolves*, without all Fear, made Havock of the *Sheep*.[20]

Similitudes, parables, analogies and exempla are central to the evangelical ardour of the Drapier's mission. Some of the most effective images are, fittingly, simple and sensational, as in the following tale from the letter *To Molesworth*:

> It is a known Story of the Dumb Boy, whose tongue forced a Passage for Speech by the Horror of seeing a Dagger at his Father's Throat. This may lessen the Wonder, that a Tradesman hid in Privacy and Silence should *cry out* when the Life and Being of his Political *Mother* are attempted before his Face; and by so infamous a Hand.[21]

Considered in the context of Swift's 'retirement', this story of induced articulation has a tempting application to his motives for reinvolvement in Irish affairs. Despite, perhaps because of, his unsettled and largely negative attitude to his birthplace, Swift wrote with more imagination, generosity and freedom than ever before. Ireland's humiliating and ambiguous relation to England provided him with a more authentic platform for righteous indignation than anything connected with his service to the Tories. His own awareness of this contrast, heard especially in the letters to Molesworth and Middleton, leads him to appreciate the necessity and virtue of a public-spirited writer and literature.

The author, like the priest, becomes the moral conscience of his audience. In his official role as Dean of St Patrick's, Swift showed his support for the Drapier by preaching against Wood's project in a sermon entitled *Doing Good*, in which he justified using the pulpit for political purposes: '. . . it is time for the pastor to cry out, that the wolf is getting into his flock, to warn them to stand together, and all to consult the common safety.'[22] As in the *Letters*, Swift here emphasises the importance of civic duty in the face of communal crisis. It would not have been lost on his audience, literary or religious, that the terms of his warning evoked the legitimate resistance to King James by Protestant Ireland only thirty years beforehand. The Drapier's audience, it should be emphasised, was limited, in his own words, to 'the True English People of Ireland', but this was the first time that colonial Ireland had expressed and seen itself imaginatively.

As in all his literary campaigns on public controversies, Swift commented on the issues in a variety of forms and disguises, many of them no more than impulsive but entertaining ephemera. On this occasion, as he had done in the role of Bickerstaff, he produced several verse-lampoons and broadsides for personal enjoyment as well as a diversion for friends.[23] He delighted in penning bogus reports for newspapers, such as the *Account of Wood's Execution*, a fantastical account of summary public justice written with gallows humour.[24] Following the fashion of solemn declarations against Wood's scheme, he even drafted one from the beggars of Dublin, who claimed they too would be financially ruined by the proposal.[25]

An important literary consequence of Swift's role as Drapier was the intervention of a young Dublin publisher and newspaper-owner, George Faulkner, who produced the first edition of *The Drapier's Letters* on 2 October 1725, only a month after the controversy was resolved. It was called *Fraud Detected: or, The Hibernian Patriot*, collecting together the five pamphlets already printed, and several pieces of verse associated with the Drapier. Ehrenpreis suggests that Swift probably helped prepare the volume.[26] Swift was so pleased with the edition that he presented a copy to the Bodleian Library, signed 'Humbly presented . . . by M. B. Drapier'. This was only the second time in his writing career that Swift had helped in a collection of his literary works, the first having been the

1711 *Miscellanies*, over a decade beforehand. The collaboration with Faulkner was one of the most momentous literary relationships formed by Swift, since this publisher was later entrusted with the only definitive edition of Swift's *Works* to be published in his lifetime.

It is a measure of Swift's imaginative energy and ambition that, during his five-month stay at Quilca, he could sustain his role as Drapier while finishing his most famous prose satire. *Gulliver's Travels* had been laid aside for the campaign against Wood (persuasive evidence itself of Swift's literary and political priorities), but had reached its first full draft while the last of the *Letters* was being prepared for the printer. In August 1725, in a single sentence of a long letter to Ford, Swift noted the conclusion of this draft with satisfaction: 'I have finished my Travells, and am now transcribing them; they are admirable Things, and will wonderfully mend the World.'[27] This optimism may well have been inspired by the popularity of the Drapier's attempts to 'mend the World' in a more realistic and familiar setting. In these early comments on his secretive satire, a clear sense of public commitment and responsibility, playful as well as serious, is regularly heard. Writing again to Ford, he describes his varied roles in the wilds of Cavan:

> We live here among a Million of wants, and where everybody is a Thief. I am amusing my self in the Quality of Bayliff to Sheridan, among Bogs and Rocks, overseeing and ranting at Irish Laborers, reading Books twice over for want of fresh ones, and fairly correcting and transcribing my Travells, for the Publick.[28]

Swift's thoughts were now turning towards London for his new book, and to a possible reunion with old friends. At the end of September 1725, he wrote to Pope, telling him that 'my Travells, in four parts Compleat' only needed a printer brave enough to publish.[29] Once the best-known propagandist and wit in England, now the most popular writer in English-speaking Ireland, Swift never sounded so confident or purposeful. Nearly sixty years of age, he tells Pope that if the satire is ever published, and his literary purpose vindicated, he could justly claim to be '...the most Indefatigable writer you have ever seen...'. The Drapier had revived Swift's faith and energy.

On 6 March 1726, the 'Hibernian Patriot' sailed from Dublin to arrange the London publication of *Gulliver's Travels*, and to enjoy a reunion with his literary friends. After five years work on the satire, he now carried a copy of his manuscript, leaving the original behind in Dublin.[30] Only a small circle of friends knew about, or had seen parts of, the story which was to become a literary sensation. Stella and Sheridan were certainly familiar with it; Bolingbroke, Vanessa and Ford had glimpsed extracts. Swift undoubtedly wanted to surprise London with his satirical fantasy, and tried to exercise some personal control over its publication. Although written entirely in Ireland, *Gulliver's Travels* was carefully arranged for an English market and audience.

When he arrived in London, he went straight to the Twickenham home of Alexander Pope, which remained his base for most of the sojourn. Swift must have enjoyed the contrast between this reception and his previous visit to London when he had to seek out lodgings for himself. He was now a famous, controversial writer and a clergyman with greater authority and independence than ever before. Besides arranging publication of his new work, he wanted to use the visit to discuss Ireland's chronic economy directly with Walpole, the Prime Minister. No doubt remembering Swift's derisive portrait of him in the Drapier's *Letter to the Whole People of Ireland*, Walpole's response to the Dean was cool and argumentative. Several of Swift's friends suspected that he was using the interviews with Walpole to sound out the prospect of an English post. Stung by the suggestion that he might be bargaining while discussing matters of principle, he wrote to Delany: 'I never set out on the foot of promotion. I have writ too many ludicrous things, have been suspected with some grounds to have writ more, and have been charged with hundreds I never writ.'[31] Swift knew that his literary reputation went before him, that the Drapier was hardly a type to be embraced by the Whig establishment. He also knew, but Walpole could not, that the author of *Gulliver's Travels* was planning a satirical revenge of outrageous proportion on English politics. Swift had few illusions about a worthy retirement in England, and told Sheridan, '. . . I am too old for new Schemes, and especially such as would bridle me in my Freedoms and Liberalities.'[32] He had neither desire nor need to crawl to London's political court. Secure in his own Dublin principality, he could now write as he pleased.

Spending most of his time socialising with Pope and Gay, it was

not until early August that Swift implemented an elaborate plan for
the publication of his book. This time, he excelled himself in the
customary strategy of impersonation by creating a deceptive set of
fictions which would serve as intermediaries with the publisher.
He first drafted an explanatory letter, then had it copied out in
Gay's hand. Posing as 'Richard Sympson', cousin of a retired
sea-captain, one Lemuel Gulliver, he offered a sample of the *Travels*
to Benjamin Motte for immediate publication:

> My cousin Mr Lemuel Gulliver entrusted me some Years ago
> with a Copy of his Travels, whereof that which I here send you is
> about a fourth part, for I shortned them very much as you will
> find in my Preface to the Reader. I have shewn them to several
> persons of great Judgement and Distinction, who are confident
> they will sell very well. And although some parts of this and the
> following Volumes may be thought in one or two places to be a
> little Satyrical, yet it is agreed they will give no offence, but in
> that you must Judge for your self, and take the Advice of your
> Friends, and if they or you be of another opinion, you may let me
> know it when you return these Papers, which I expect shall be in
> three Days at furthest.[33]

The fictional cousin delegates critical evaluation to other, unnamed
persons 'of great Judgement and Distinction', thereby authenticat-
ing his good standing as a mere go-between. Enjoying the role of a
simple, realistic businessman, he asks for a down-payment of two
hundred pounds, part of the money to go to a special fund for
retired seamen. Sympson says someone, but not himself, will come
to the publisher's office 'at 9 a clock at night on Thursday' to
receive a written response. If Motte agrees to publish, each of the
remaining three parts of the book will be delivered separately
during the following week, and an unnamed messenger will collect
the money on the night of the first delivery.

The unsuspecting Motte fell in with this stealthy intrigue, and
promptly agreed to publish. However, he could not meet the
drastic deadlines for payment or publication, pointing out that the
summer was 'the most dead Season of the Year'. He suggested
publication within a month of receiving the full text, and payment
within six months, obviously hoping the sales would cover his
outlay. Two days after Motte's reply, a single-sentence note was
delivered to Motte, reading, 'I would have both Volumes come out

together and published by Christmas at furthest', and signed
'R. Sympson'. Two days later, on 15 August, his hoax complete,
Swift left London. The *Dublin Gazette,* in a style usually reserved for
royalty, announced his return with headlines of 'Long live the
Drapier!'.

Outwardly, Swift's *Travels* would not have come as a surprise to
its readers: but his parody of a familiar genre soon proved quite
shocking. Travel literature was one of the most popular genres in
the early eighteenth century.[34] In an age of discovery and adven-
ture, when other cultures were being compared to Europe's,
narratives of this kind could be both moralistic and fantastic. Swift
uses these conventions to ridicule European pretensions, but
without romanticising primitivism. He also has a more specific,
and contemporary, target in mind. While the landscapes of his
Travels are figuratively remote, Gulliver's journeying almost coin-
cides with Swift's literary and political career up to his appointment as Dean. Gulliver first sets out in 1699, returns home for good
in 1716, and begins his account in 1720. In other words, his
memoirs represent Swift's simultaneous recollection of English
politics.

Scholars generally agree that *Gulliver's Travels* is not inspired by,
or modelled on, any particular narrative. Swift's fondness for travel
books, as evidenced by those in his own library,[35] suggests that the
idea of a fantastic voyage might have come from some of his
reading, such as Dampier's *New Voyage round the World* (1697), or
Cyrano de Bergerac's *Histoire de la Lune* (1656) and *Histoire du Soleil*
(1661). The spirit and style of his satire is obviously enriched by his
wide, mostly classical, reading. But the search for meaning
through sources is often as speculative as the decipherment of
contemporary allusions. Radical in form, conservative in outlook,
the *Travels* achieve a universal form of allegory which includes a
sustained contemporary satire.

Gulliver's Travels has never ceased to stimulate and attract
controversial interpretation. The most extraordinary aspect of the
book is the tension between its structural simplicity and its
thematic ambiguity. Critics have always agreed on the most
obvious feature of the narrative: Swift's intention to satirise the
contradictions of contemporary English politics through Gulliver's
embarrassing attempts to justify them to the uninitiated and the
innocent. This kind of understanding is usually based on the first
two voyages, to Lilliput and Brobdingnag. But Swift clearly in-

tended much more than a veiled swipe at the contemporary Whig interest, and pushed Gulliver into areas of experience and meaning which could never be read with such assurance or security. Parts III and IV, to Laputa and the land of the Houyhnhnms, retain stylistic and circumstantial features of the earlier voyages, but raise elemental and universal questions of identity and significance which transform the textual character of the whole narrative. While most critics in the eighteenth and nineteenth centuries argued over the morality or sanity of the composition, twentieth-century critics have uncovered a text with no fixed meaning, an ingeniously 'open' text remarkable for its fictive ambiguity. Now considered as the most 'modern' of Swift's writings, a metafiction which needs to be protected from reductionist readings, *Gulliver's Travels* has gone through and survived every possible critical approach. It might be argued that only *after* Freud and Saussure could its potential depth be sounded.

Yet even the most heavily intellectualised reading of the *Travels* will recognise its graphic, physical immediacy. At every stage of Gulliver's Odyssey, the flesh is a signal for the spirit. The realist and the materialist in Swift never allow Gulliver to transcend or forget the corporeal world, even when, as with the Houyhnhnms, he is most desperate to become pure intellect. If there is an obsessive mind behind the *Travels*, it is also one which continually humbles and mortifies Gulliver through showing him that the body is as much a prison-house as language.

On the other hand, the physical imagery of the fiction, symmetrical and systematic, is often as farcical as it is tragic. Always a master of his readers' response, Swift arranges the first two voyages as a complimentary pair of contrasting experiences based on human scale: no matter what dimension or proportion Gulliver assumes, his moral stature remains inflexible. By the end of the story, when he tries to walk like a horse, the relation between human and animal, intellect and body, civilisation and primitivism, has become much more ambiguous. We know Gulliver's attitude towards the Houyhnhnms, but what of Swift's? How should the reader respond to an ideal of human rationality figured in animal form? Is Gulliver's final conversion to the contemplative life evidence of enlightenment or insanity? When, if ever, can this text be trusted? This calculated and stealthy confusion of categories normally held apart by civil and religious society is at the centre of Swift's strategy throughout the *Travels*. A few years later, he would distil this art into the horror of *A Modest Proposal.*

Part of what contributes to the 'modern' feel of *Gulliver's Travels* is Swift's fictional distance from the text and his substitution of a narrator who is also the author of that text. Questions of reliability, distortion, subjectivity and interpretation immediately enter any critical discourse which acknowledges Swift's manipulation of a persona who always professes good faith. Gulliver's tale is that of a survivor, someone who has been rescued, however unwillingly, from a series of nightmarish experiences which have profoundly affected his sense of what is 'natural'. His story ends on a note of nostalgia for the 'wise and virtuous Houyhnhnms' who now haunt his disturbed memory of that ideal. An outcast from his own culture, Gulliver comes to resemble 'alienated' Man, an individual unable to accept or forgive his own kind.

While allowing for the legitimacy of such a philosophical interpretation, we do well to remember the detailed authorial self-justification with which Swift provides Gulliver at the conclusion of the tale. Much of the detail suggests the pamphleteering Swift come to the rhetorical assistance of his puppet. Gulliver insists that his 'sole Intention was the PUBLICK GOOD', that unless writers instruct as well as entertain they are doomed to oblivion, and that he wrote his own account 'without any View towards Profit or Praise'. Preacher, writer and narrator join voices in denouncing 'Pride' as the greatest obstacle to human understanding, while celebrating the Houyhnhnms' cultivation of 'Friendship and Benevolence' above all other virtues. Such praise might sound sentimental if it were not for the trials which its speaker has endured.

Gulliver's Travels contains Swift's pamphleteering energy, but is free of the immediacy of meaning which that form usually demands. It is a 'mature' work composed with great stylistic care over several years. In its scale, self-sufficiency, formal elaboration and imaginative adventurism, it is not typical of Swift's literary career. A rare form of imaginative indulgence, it is a magnificent, but freakish, monument to his otherwise short artistic fuse.

No matter how we interpret the *Travels*, the allegory and the satire are linked by Swift's uncompromising rejection of contemporary civilisation. Seen alongside his earliest satires, written nearly twenty-five years beforehand, we can detect the same kind of extreme orthodoxy which exposes the present corruption and betrayal of classical civilisation. In terms of Swift's literary career, the *Travels* belong to his many writings in defence of tradition. This protective stance views the present as an increasingly gross perversion of an idealised past. The imagery of animalism and the manner of disgust belong to a vision of incorrigible decadence. When Gulliver visits Glubbdubdrib, the island of sorcerors and magicians, he uses the occasion to summon up the spirits of the classical world. He then spends an entire day enjoying the company of 'those Ancients, who were most renowned for Wit and Learning'. When he asks his necromantic hosts to conjure up the spirits of 'the modern Dead, who had made the greatest Figure for two or three Hundred Years past in our own and other Countries of Europe', the noble spectacle turns into a freak-show:

> I was chiefly disgusted with modern History. For having strictly examined all the Persons of greatest Name in the Courts of Princes for an Hundred Years past, I found how the World had been misled by prostitute Writers, to ascribe the greatest Exploits in War to Cowards, the wisest Counsel to Fools, Sincerity to Flatterers, *Roman* Virtue to Betrayers of their Country, Piety to Atheists, Chastity to Sodomites, Truth to Informers.[36]

One of the most paradoxical attractions about Swift, and especially true of his *Travels*, is that such despair and loathing should find such energetic, affirmative expression. The perspective is bitterly pessimistic, yet the style always suggests a possibility of redemption. Swift may have found the world intolerable but, like the Drapier, he could never keep quiet about it. *Gulliver's Travels* is the work of a writer with just enough hope to believe in the value of communication with a fallen world.

On 28 October 1726, Motte published *Travels Into Several Remote Nations of the World*, in two octavo volumes, selling at eight shillings and sixpence. A fortnight after publication, Swift began to receive a series of congratulatory letters from his Scriblerian friends expressing surprise and delight at the popularity of the daring satire. Although he had stayed with Pope and Gay, he had not revealed the story to them. John Arbuthnot wrote that the *Travels* 'will have as great a Run as John Bunian'. Responding more immediately to the humour than to the severity of the tale, he congratulated Swift on writing 'such a merry work'.[37] Pope, still working on *The Dunciad*, confirmed the popular but controversial reception of the *Travels* in London. He assured Swift that the

'particular reflections' on known individuals were very effectively
disguised and could not make the author liable to prosecution.
Since most people, including himself, saw it as a general satire on
humanity, he was perplexed at the Dean's extreme caution.[38] The
most enthusiastic congratulations came from Gay, who wrote:

> About ten days ago a Book was publish'd here of the Travels of
> one Gulliver, which hath been the conversation of the whole
> Town ever since: The whole impression sold in a week; and
> nothing is more diverting than to hear the different opinions
> people give of it, though all agree in liking it extremely. 'Tis
> generally said that you are the Author, but I am told, the
> Bookseller declares he knows not from what hand it came. From
> the highest to the lowest it is universally read, from the Cabinet
> council to the Nursery. The Politicians to a man agree, that it is
> free from particular reflections, but that the Satire on general
> societies of men is too severe.[39]

He added several other impressions, including ironic surprise
about Bolingbroke's response, 'the person who least approves it'.
(Swift must have smiled.) It comes as quite a surprise to hear Gay
regret that Swift has not yet seen the publication he wrote.
Adopting the humour of the absent author, he recommends the
book highly, and promises to send him a copy.

But Swift had already seen a printed copy of the book and found
that Motte had taken many unauthorised liberties with the text.[40]
Now began a most complicated, confused and lengthy process of
correcting the first edition. Most of the typographical blunders in
this edition may be attributed to the fact that Motte worked from a
copy of the original, but not one in Swift's handwriting. The
copyist may well have made errors which Swift had not time to
correct, and which the printer reproduced in good faith. The
original manuscript, of course, had never left Ireland. To compli-
cate matters even further, a separate printer was sub-contracted by
Motte for each of the four parts of the text. Writing from Dublin at
the end of November, Swift thanked Pope for his appreciation of
the *Travels*, but complained of 'several passages which appear to be
patched and altered', especially in the second volume.[41] The
grossest alteration to the text was the deletion of several pages
from the Voyage to Laputa, which contained an allegorical account
of the Drapier's campaign against Wood.[42] Motte, understandably,

did not want to remind the Law how the Drapier's printer had been treated. Faced with a travestied edition, Swift decided to begin the formidable task of arranging an authoritative text.

But while he was sifting through his papers and the disfigured first edition, the book was selling so well that two more octavo editions were published in London before the end of 1726, each one selling over two thousand copies. Early in the New Year, Motte brought out a duodecimo edition with illustrations. In major as well as minor aspects, this was not the book which Swift had written. Trying to resume control of his work, he asked his friend, Charles Ford, while on a visit to Dublin, to assist in the preparation of a list of corrections to be sent to London.

Because Swift exercised no legal control over the first three editions, the *Travels* soon became public and international property, turned into a myriad shapes.[43] Two London newspapers immediately began a reprint of their own in serialised form. Prose summaries and guides were published, including a 'Key' by Swift's old enemy, Edmund Curll, who had exploited the popularity of *A Tale Of A Tub* in the same way, over twenty years beforehand. Two French translations appeared in early 1727, followed by Dutch and German editions. Like some of his own literary heroes, Rabelais and Cervantes, Swift had become a writer of European repute. Yet there was still no authorised or definitive edition of this best-seller. Swift's strategy of delegation, silence and removal was partly responsible for this uncontrollable situation: by first pretending he had not written the book, and by returning to Dublin to miss its publication, he had forfeited authorial control.

However, while London had the book, Dublin had the writer. Two Dublin editions, both based on Motte, were printed shortly after the first London edition. One of these was by John Hyde, a printer Swift had previously used to publish the Dublin edition of his *Conduct of the Allies* and Prior's *Poems*. Living in the same city as this experienced printer meant that Swift could work alongside the edition. Such collaboration, of course, was a unique feature of Hyde's duodecimo volume, whose title-page declared, 'In this Impression, several Errors in the London Edition are corrected.' (Swift's copy of Hyde's edition, the only early edition corrected by the author himself, has come to be known as the 'Armagh' copy, ever since it was first recognised and examined by scholars during the 1930s in the public library of that city.[44]) Hyde's edition assumes its real significance later on in Swift's career, when

Faulkner used it for his authoritative edition of 1735, which Swift approved. Thus, a more fully corrected (but still incomplete) edition of *Gulliver's Travels* took almost ten years.

A few months after the *Travels* first appeared, Swift decided to visit London once more. He wanted to tackle Motte about the profits from his book. In February, he wrote to Knightley Chetwode:

> . . . I believe it will be the last journey I shall ever take thither, but the omission of some matters last summer, by the absence of certain people, hath made it necessary. As to Captain Gulliver, I find his book is very much censured in this kingdom which abounds in excellent judges; but in England I hear it hath made a bookseller almost rich enough to be an alderman.[45]

The 'absence of certain people' refers to the son and friends of the Earl of Oxford, whom Swift wished to consult for his *History of the Four Last Years of the Queen*, a publishing fixation not yet satisfied. He also wanted to discuss with Pope a volume of *Miscellanies*, mostly verse, which would be their first collaborative literary project. On 9 April, he set off on a second, six-month visit to London. As he suspected, it would indeed be his last journey to England.

As with the previous year's visit, he stayed in Twickenham, and from there began his literary errands. Motte had received Ford's list of corrections for the *Travels*, and Swift had delivered a special preface for the next edition. This was entitled, 'A Letter from Capt. Gulliver to his Cousin Sympson', in which the fictitious author berated his cousin for permitting such a botched version of his story to be published. On 4 May 1727, Motte duly published his 'Second Edition, Corrected'. Far from improving the text, this edition was even worse than the first one. Old errors were left uncorrected, new typographical blunders sprouted, none of the censored passages were restored, and the 'Letter' did not appear.[46] Motte, of course, did not want to include a preface which scorned his professional efficiency. As if to complete his defiance of the author's wishes, Motte included a selection of Pope's Gulliverian verse in the edition, as a commercial novelty. This 'Second Edition, Corrected' was no more than a sorry version of the first edition, a disastrous episode in Swift's lifelong argument with commercial publishers.

After the rather mixed fortunes of *Gulliver's Travels*, Swift faced a series of personal and literary disappointments. Nobody, especially Oxford's son, seemed interested in the publication of his *History*, a manuscript he had so carefully prepared and guarded. He had also been planning a celebratory tour of France, having received a flattering and enthusiastic invitation from Voltaire, who was staying in London that summer. But when King George died, in June, Swift hesitated. The Monarch's death, argued Swift's friends, would create a new political administration which might reward former allies. Swift also heard frightening news from Dublin about Stella's health, and was engaged in a tense correspondence with friends at home, urging remedies and demanding daily bulletins on her illness. In June, the French translator of *Gulliver's Travels*, L'Abbé des Fontaines, offered Swift a copy of his two-volume, abridged edition, and a shamefaced letter apologising for his criticisms of the author in the preface, and for his censorship of the text.[47] He pleaded that he had been obliged to 'adapt' the text to suit French taste and circumstance. Swift replied bluntly:

> . . . le bon gout est le meme par tout ou il y a des gens d'esprit, de judgement et de Scavoir. si donc les livres de Sieur Gulliver ne sont calcules que pour les Isles Britanniques, ce voyageur doit passer pour un tres pitoyable Ecrivain. les memes vices, et les memes folles regnent par tout, du moins, dans tous les pays civilises de l'Europe, et l'auteur qui n'ecrit que pour une ville, une province, un Royaune, ou meme un siecle, merite si peu d'être traduit qu'il ne merite pas d'être lû.[48]

This is one of Swift's clearest declarations of literary and moral idealism. Linguistic and cultural differences should be of no account between people of taste. For someone whose sense of civilisation was mediated entirely through Latin and Greek, Swift found des Fontaines' reasoning absurd. If poor Gulliver could transcend linguistic barriers and learn something from other and earlier civilisations, surely men of letters could do the same. The Frenchman, not Gulliver, is the untranslatable provincial.

During this summer of 1727, Swift, almost in sympathy with the dying Stella, suffered constantly from fits of giddiness and deafness. In late August, expecting the worst news from Dublin, he wrote to Sheridan, begging him '. . . to tell me no Particulars, but the Event in general: My Weakness, my Age, my Friendship will

bear no more.' In September, afraid of opening Sheridan's replies
and bracing himself to come home, he wrote again:

> ... it would have been a Reproach to me to be in perfect Health,
> when such a Friend is desperate. I do profess, upon my
> Salvation, that the distressed and desperate Condition of our
> Friend, makes Life so indifferent to me, who by Course of Nature
> have so little left, that I do not think it worth the Time to
> struggle.[49]

Mortified by his own illness, riven by the prospect of Stella's death,
Swift left Pope's house on 18 September, without notice, and
started home.

After some confusion, he decided to sail from Holyhead. Having
missed one boat, and foul weather preventing the next from
sailing, the Dean and his new servant, Jack Watt, settled down in
the local inn for a farcical and humiliating epilogue to his last
English visit. Without anything to read, Swift started to write to
Stella in a small notebook, now known as the *Holyhead Journal*.[50]
Resuming the relaxed, anecdotal and intimate style of his former
Journal to Stella, he gave a daily account of his wretched week in
this barbarous outpost. Even Swift's dignity could not prevent him
from seeing the irony of his plight – the author of *Gulliver's Travels*
stranded amongst a people who spoke an unintelligible language,
reduced to squabbling with Watt about weather and lousy bed-
linen. He moaned, 'In short: I come from being used like an
Emperor to be used worse than a dog at Holyhead.' There was
none of his favourite wine left at the inn, as the Irish passengers on
the previous boat had finished it off before sailing. Watt, 'whose
blunders would bear an history', had forgotten to pack any fresh
shirts for his master, who was terrified of catching the mange.
Swift had very disturbing dreams, 'an abundance of nonsense', in
which he repeatedly fell off his horse. The utter isolation and
primitivism of the situation somehow suited his foreboding mood,
however, as he looked across the Irish Sea to catch sight of the
Wicklow Hills. Compared with the triumphant return of the
Drapier the previous summer, this time Swift felt grim and
vindictive. He wrote four poems during the week, all of them on
the horror of life in Ireland:

Remove me from this land of slaves,
Where all are fools, and all are knaves;
Where every knave and fool is bought,
Yet kindly sells himself for naught;
Where Whig and Tory fiercely fight
Who's in the wrong, who in the right;
And when their country lies at stake
They only fight for fighting's sake,
Where English sharpers take the pay,
And then stand by to see fair play.[51]

This is the indignant Drapier in rhyme. Swift's violent despair, here blackened by emotion as much as by conviction, is also at the heart of *Gulliver's Travels*.

After the two greatest literary triumphs of his career, within a year of each other, something in Swift's imagination contracted. The champion of Ireland's freedom, the greatest contemporary satirist in the English language, a writer of European fame, he now began a retreat from public affairs, and prepared for desolation.

6

'I have stretched out my Hand, and no Man regarded'

Swift came home to watch Stella die. Only a few months were left to a friendship which had begun over thirty years beforehand. The evening Stella died, Swift immediately began a private character of his dearest companion:

> This day, being Sunday, January 28th, 1727–8, about eight o'clock at night, a servant brought me a note, with an account of the death of the truest, most virtuous, and valuable friend, that I, or perhaps any other person ever was blessed with. She expired about six in the evening of this day; and, as soon as I am left alone, which is about eleven at night, I resolve, for my own satisfaction, to say something of her life and character.[1]

During the next three days, while the funeral arrangements were being made, Swift wrote a dignified and tender story of Stella's character and distinction. Above all, he praised her for acceptability into serious, male company, 'the usual topics of ladies discourse being such as she had little knowledge of, and less relish'. The paternal and tutorial nature of the friendship is heard in his praise of attributes which mirror his own principles and taste: he approves of her simplicity of expression, her prudent management of money, her intolerance of fools, and her patriotism. As someone who shared the life of a writer, she is also remembered as intelligent and discriminating company:

> She had a true taste of wit and good sense, both in poetry and prose, and was a perfect good critic of style: Neither was it easy to find a more proper or impartial judge, whose advice an author might better rely on, if he intended to send a thing into the

world, provided it was on a subject that came within the compass of her knowledge.[2]

Stella's practical and intellectual assistance to Swift, as audience, amanuensis, and model of virtuous friendship, should not be underestimated.

On the day of her funeral, he was too ill to attend, but continued to write about her, moving into another room to avoid seeing the lights from the cathedral. In the letters preserved from this period, Swift never once mentions his loss and grief, but when we look at the complexion of most of his writings after this tragedy, we may agree with Ehrenpreis when he remarks that Swift's 'real life was over'.[3]

After the success of *The Drapier's Letters* and *Gulliver's Travels*, Swift tried to consolidate his literary reputation through a collaborative project with Pope, one which would assemble and organise an authoritative selection of their writings. Now in his sixties, he wanted to preserve the best of his work in a properly supervised edition, as much to avoid pirated versions of his writing as to celebrate his friendship with the English poet. Swift entrusted Pope with the task of collecting and editing material for a set of *Miscellanies* to be published by Motte in London. Although the project was conceived as a monument to a very special kind of literary friendship, it soon became clear that it served Pope's interests more than those of Swift who, watching the affair from Dublin, felt yet again that his work was beyond his personal control.

The first two volumes of these *Miscellanies* were published in June 1727, and Pope had plans for a third volume to be published as quickly as possible, to be entitled *The Last Volume*, in order to outmanoeuvre pirate editions. Writing to Motte at the end of the year, in response to the publisher's queries about possible illustrations for future editions of the *Travels*,[4] Swift remarks that most of the material in the two volumes is drawn from his poetry, a fact which both pleased and surprised him. He says, 'There is all the Poetry I ever writ worth printing,' and reminds Motte that Pope will have the final say about the forthcoming volume, '. . . and I will take his judgement'. In January 1728, Pope wrote enthusiastically to Swift about his latest work, *The Dunciad*, which was to be a centre-piece for *The Last Volume*.[5] In the letter, he copied out those lines from his poem which paid tribute to the Dean, and appealed to him to 'consider, re-consider, criticize, hyper-criticize, and consult with Sheridan, Delany, and all the Literati . . . to render it less unworthy of you.' To remind Swift of the Scriblerian dimension to all this literary activity, he wrote that their mutual friend, Gay, was finished with his *Beggar's Opera*, which 'is just on the point of Delivery'.[6] Swift must have been heartened by Pope's work, but his own contribution to the next volume was becoming a chore. In February, he wrote again to Motte,[7] complaining that many of the poems he had been searching for were missing or lost. Transacting a collaborative project through the post had led to misunderstandings with Pope, who returned some of Swift's verses, mistakenly believing them to be merely translations and therefore unsuitable. Other verses were returned unapproved, but Swift, surprisingly, did not demur. He repeated his wish that all his work 'must be shown to Mr Pope and Mr Gay and not published without their approbation'. This reliance on Pope was not matched by his friend's reliability: *The Last Volume* appeared in March, but without *The Dunciad*, which Pope published separately two months later. Now began a serious and secretive reconsideration, on Swift's side, of how to ensure a more authoritative and personalised edition of his literary works.

On Pope's side, friendship and self-interest combined to extend his venture with Swift to yet another volume, to be called, rather confusingly, *The Third Volume*. This time, however, Swift's response was deliberately slow and evasive. Pope had to wait almost four years before Swift posted a variety of prose and verse for this final volume. In June 1732, he wrote to Pope about his lack of inspiration, 'a Rhime with me is almost as hard to find as a Guinea', and reminded him that many of the prose tracts he had written were of local Irish interest and unsuited to a London readership.[8] In October, *The Third Volume* eventually appeared, and the *Miscellanies* were complete. Although both Pope and Motte were now in control of much of Swift's literary canon, and looked set to assume responsibility for any definitive edition, Swift outlived and outwitted such expectations.

Physical or emotional suffering never silenced Swift completely. On the contrary, he always found some way of giving literary expression to moods which might seem incompatible with invention. On Stella's death, his instinct and need was to formalise his response immediately. On less tragic, or simply frustrating, occasions, such as the chaos at Holyhead, he fought against the desolation with the imaginative consolation of some narrative. Swift found it hard not to write: in a crisis, he usually reached for a pen. He also seems to have preserved a clear and strict separation of private and public responsibilities, even when both attracted his literary talent. While recovering from the trauma of Stella's death, he maintained a full business-correspondence on the *Miscellanies*, discussed yet another collaborative literary project (this time with Sheridan), and turned towards the last phase of his pamphleteering crusade on Ireland.

A few weeks after Stella's funeral, Swift wrote and published two anonymous pamphlets, both printed by Sarah Harding. The first of these, *A Short View of the State of Ireland*, appeared on 19 March, and attacked those who pretended that Ireland enjoyed normality and prosperity. Without resorting to either a fictional mask or dramatic persona, he savaged English place-men and Irish absentees who thrived off a population's degradation and sacrificed conscience to ambition. His bitter sense of injustice and isolation is expressed in enumerative fashion and, more effectively, summarised in a domestic metaphor – 'Thus, we are in the Condition of Patients, who have Physick sent to them by Doctors at a Distance, Strangers to their Constitution, and the Nature of their Disease.'[9] He mimics the fawning reports of observers afraid to tell the truth, but then confesses 'my Heart is too heavy to continue this Irony longer'. Aware that remedies for Ireland's condition were usually drawn from other, normal economies which enjoyed political freedom, he summarises his contempt for such pseudo-scientific benevolence with parodic bluntness – 'There is not one Argument used to prove the Riches of Ireland, which is not a logical Demonstration of its Poverty'. Here begins Swift's figure of Ireland as a barbaric distortion of Nature and Reason.

Less than a week after the *Short View* appeared, Swift published *An Answer to a Paper called a Memorial*, the first of a series of 'Answers' to pamphlets by individual reformers who often wrote with Swift in mind or sent them to him for pre-publication approval. The speed and urgency with which Swift could compose such responses is indicated by the fact that the *Memorial* was published only days before Swift's reply. This *Memorial* was yet another economic proposal to solve Ireland's crisis, this time by raising a huge public fund to import food during the frequent

famines. It was composed by John Browne, a character known to
Swift since the days of the Drapier's campaign, when Browne had
testified to Wood's reliability and integrity, provoking the Drapier
to vilify Browne as a traitor to his country.[10] Before writing his
pamphlet, Browne had taken the extraordinary step of writing to
the Dean asking for forgiveness and pledging his good faith – a
remarkable sign of Swift's authority in matters of public
controversy.[11] Swift's *Answer* is one of the most bitter and violent
responses to philanthropy he ever wrote, an ironic reaction since it
was precisely his work as the Drapier which had inspired so many
imitators. Caught between a principled belief in the need for
public-spirited writing and a weary despair of its effectiveness, his
expression becomes increasingly apocalyptic and brutal, the confident reason and playful wit of earlier pamphlets giving way to
assertions dramatised through grotesque imagery. His *Answer*,
ignoring the detailed calculations of the *Memorial*, is dominated by
the image of a land where people are displaced by animals.
Converting land from tillage to pasture resulted in 'this prodigious
Plenty of Cattle, and Dearth of human Creatures', a situation
which defied common sense and offended reason. Raising money
in a country without any, importing food into a country which
discouraged tillage, was a scheme 'as vain as that of Rabelais,
which was to squeeze out Wind from the Posteriors of a dead Ass'.
Impatience is goaded into sadism as Swift admits to a 'malicious
Pleasure' in watching his warning ignored and his predictions
confirmed. Only the chilling derision of a vengeful Jeremiah can
adequately express his sense of outrage:

> *Wisdom crieth in the Streets; because I have called and ye refused; I have*
> *stretched out my Hand, and no Man regarded. But ye have set at nought*
> *my Counsel, and would none of my Reproof. I also will laugh at your*
> *Calamity, and mock when your Fear cometh.*[12]

Such a forbidding rhetoric reminds us of the clergyman behind the
writer, a dual personality who now viewed human stupidity with
the same kind of contempt as the prophet felt for a people who
rejected salvation.

In May 1728, Swift began an unusual collaborative project with
his clerical friend, Sheridan, which allowed him to indulge his role
of public observer and critic in a more relaxed and less strident
style than in the tracts. This was the *Intelligencer*, a weekly paper

which ran from May to December. Modelled on London papers like the *Examiner* and the *Guardian*, but without their kind of party allegiance, its aim was 'to gather Materials enough to Inform, or Divert, or Correct, or Vex the Town'.[13] Unlike the joint venture with Pope and the *Miscellanies*, this had no such formal literary pretensions or expectations. Work with Sheridan was usually playful, witty and spontaneous, and the *Intelligencer* allowed Swift freedom to indulge more personal, even more whimsical, subjects in prose than in the demanding and competitive alliance with Pope. Beyond the pressure of literary London, the *Intelligencer* was aimed at the smaller, more intimate, colonial audience in Georgian Dublin.

Swift contributed seven articles to the paper (one of which was a reprint of his *Short View*) on a range of topics, including the economy, education, clericalism and public satirists. In the third issue, he wrote an energetic and sympathetic defence of Gay's *Beggar's Opera*, which had achieved unprecedented success on the London stage. Gay had sent his friend a personal copy of the printed text in March, a gesture which delighted Swift. It was unusual for him to enthuse about anything to do with the theatre, but Gay's public-spirited satire and the Scriblerian bond between the two men inspired Swift to write one of his rare exercises in textual evaluation. Characteristically, he used Gay's play as an exemplary kind of satire which showed its concern for society by exposing its abuses. Swift applauded the play's humour for being 'natural' rather than refined, and dismissed his fellow-clergymen who, regarding the play as offensive, confused method with purpose. In its own way, the *Beggar's Opera* seemed to complement Swift's *Travels* as an entertaining fiction designed to expose vice and strengthen morality. Swift concluded his essay in forthright, provocative terms:

> Upon the whole, I deliver my Judgement, that nothing but servile Attachment to a Party, Affectation of Singularity, lament-able Dullness, mistaken Zeal, or studied Hypocrisy, can have the least reasonable Objection against this excellent moral Perform-ance of the *Celebrated* Mr Gay.[14]

During this period, Swift saw himself as part of a satirical triumvi-rate, led by himself and the *Travels*, and followed by Gay's *Opera* and Pope's *Dunciad*. He had written to Gay, 'The Beggars Opera

hath knockt down Gulliver, I hope to see Popes Dullness knock
down the Beggars Opera.' In the same letter he confidently
underlined the value of such satires, stating that 'two or three such
trifles every year to expose vice and make people laugh with
innocency does more publick Service than all the Ministers of State
from Adam to Walpole.'[15] It is noteworthy that he never expressed
any comparable faith in his Irish writings: England was corrupt,
but it was not a hopeless case. Abuses in the English political
system could be exposed, opposed, even corrected by a literature
committed to the public welfare. If the writer on English affairs
might be viewed as a literary surgeon, his Irish counterpart could
be seen only as a pathologist.

In June 1728, shortly after the *Intelligencer* first appeared, Swift
travelled north to Markethill, near Armagh, to spend the first of
three successive summers in the company of Sir Arthur and Lady
Acheson.[16] This rural interlude, in the company of distinguished
colonial gentry, inspired some of his most accomplished and
playful verse on the virtues of friendship and sociability. The spirit
of the 'Markethill poems' is in extreme contrast to the violent and
jaded character of much of his pamphleteering during the same
period, suggesting, yet again, that Swift turned to poetry for a
special kind of private, imaginative release. Tired of haranguing an
increasingly unresponsive public, he enjoyed a poetic holiday.

Lady Acheson became the subject and persona of much of his
poetry at Markethill, allowing Swift to resume a favourite role of
paternal tutor dedicated to the improvement of a woman's character. The most distinctive feature of these poems is their teasing
mimicry of the lady's private thoughts concerning her clerical
guest, a device which also allows Swift to reveal a critical and
comic self-portrait. In 'My Lady's Lamentation and Complaint
against the Dean', the tormented hostess tells of the visitor's
exhausting regime of exercise, diet, gardening and reading, one
which has disturbed her usual pattern of leisurely self-indulgence:

> At breakfast he'll ask
> An account of my task,
> Put a word out of joint,
> He rages and frets,
> His manners forgets;
> And, as I am serious,
> Is very imperious.

> No book for delight
> Must come in my sight;
> But, instead of new plays,
> Dull Bacon's Essays,
> And pore ev'ry day on
> That nasty Pantheon.[17]

Through Lady Acheson, Swift pictures himself as a benevolent, somewhat eccentric tyrant whose spartan energy is the jest of the neighbourhood. In *Journal of a Modern Lady*, speaking in his own voice, Swift confronts her charge that he is a 'woman-hater', and proceeds to justify his meddling presence by showing how Lady Acheson's leisure hours are spent in compulsive gambling, late nights and gossip.[18] On his second visit, in the summer of 1729, he became so attached to the place that he seriously thought of building a country house on a site to be called 'Drapier's Hill', and promptly poeticised his ambition:

> That when a Nation long enslav'd,
> Forgets by whom it once was sav'd;
> When none the DRAPIER's Praise shall sing;
> His Signs aloft no longer swing;
> His Medals and his Prints forgotten,
> And all his Handkerchiefs are rotten;
> His famous LETTERS made waste Paper;
> This Hill may keep the Name of Drapier.[19]

By his third visit, Swift sensed that Sir Arthur no longer welcomed his literary guest. Sorry to leave the enjoyable company of Lady Acheson, who delighted in the poetic badinage, but realising the impropriety of staying on, Swift formally concluded his visit with 'The Dean's Reasons for not building at Drapier's Hill', a witty but sombre account of a spoiled friendship. In the poem, Swift contrasts the reclusive personality of his scholarly host with his own earthy, convivial manner, and describes an incompatibility of taste and interest which gives us a lesser-known and therefore surprising self-image:

> My spirits with my body progging,
> Both hand in hand together jogging;
> Sunk over head and ears in matter,

> Nor can of metaphysics smatter;
> Am more diverted with a quibble
> Than dreams of worlds intelligible;
> And think all notions too abstracted
> Are like the ravings of a crakt head.[20]

The baronet is pictured as mirthless company, someone too lifeless to enjoy 'material' pleasure and distraction. The Dean's humour is social, immediate and whimsical. Offended by Acheson's frigidity, Swift concludes his valediction with a common-sense question: 'For, why should I continue still/To serve a friend against his will?' Friendship always released Swift's most witty and skilful literary instincts. The most enduring kind of love, he delighted in giving it formal, ceremonial and elaborate expression.

During these years which included the visits to Markethill, Swift engaged in prolific correspondence with his old literary friends in London, as if to balance his rural and provincial seclusion with a reminder of his distinguished metropolitan contacts. As well as the usual documentary value and interest of his letters, describing life with the Achesons, they are often eloquent and intimate reflections on his convictions and feelings. In February 1729, on hearing the news that his old friend, Congreve, had died, he wrote to Pope lamenting the death of one 'whom I loved from my youth', and wondered if it were better to be friendless in the face of such a prospect, as if companionship ensured grief.[21] Now approaching old age, Swift often confides a retrospective view of his literary career, telling Pope that 'all my endeavours from a boy to distinguish my self, were only for want of a great Title and Fortune,' but that now 'the reputation of wit or great learning does the office of a blue riband, or of a coach and six horses.'[22] With his usual clarity and directness, he tells Pope that 'To be remembered for ever on the account of our friendship, is what would exceedingly please me.'[23] Pope, who kept promising to visit Swift in Ireland (but never did) became quite rhapsodic about his friendship with the elderly Dean. In October 1728, he wrote that the *Dunciad* was the result of Swift's inspiration, 'since certainly without you it had never been. Would to God we were together for the rest of our lives!'[24] In a most self-conscious letter to Swift, in November 1729, Pope raises the inevitable question of the 'literary' significance of correspondence between famous writers:

Now as I love you better than most I have ever met with in the world, and esteem you too the more the longer I have compar'd you with the rest of the world; so inevitably I write to you more negligently, that is more openly, and what all but such as love another will call writing worse. I smile to think how Curl would be bit, were our Epistles to fall into his hands, and how gloriously they would fall short of every ingenious reader's expectations?[25]

Pope's crafted emphasis on the spontaneity of his letters is not entirely convincing. Combining a unique literary talent with shrewd understanding of the literary market, he was determined to enhance his own reputation through editorial control of Swift's occasional writings. Still working on the *Third Volume* of his *Miscellanies*, he managed to obtain copies of most of the Markethill poems for inclusion, though Swift did not always share his enthusiasm.[26]

Although Swift himself now realised the difficulty of preserving a 'private' dimension to his writing, especially his letters, he also knew that public vanity was not confined to politicians. On the significance of a literary correspondence, he wrote to Pope:

I find you have been a writer of Letters almost from your infancy, and by your own confession had Schemes even then of Epistolary fame. Montaigne says that if he could have excelled in any kind of writing, it would have been in Letters; but I doubt that they would not have been naturally, for it is plain that all Pliny's Letters were written with a view of publishing, and I accuse Voltaire himself of the same crime, although he be an Author I am fond of. They cease to be Letters when they become a jeu d'esprit.[27]

For Swift, pretending to be private was a distortion of friendship which resulted in an inferior, because affected, style. This sounds like a warning to the younger poet from the ageing satirist whose current complaint is the misattribution or exploitation of literature by adventurers. Pope replied to Swift's insinuation, denying the charge of 'Epistolary fame', but conceding his desire to publish a volume of their correspondence 'for my own secret satisfaction', and as a tribute to their friendship.[28] Although Swift was never shy of talking about the importance of money (he told Bolingbroke that 'Oeconomy . . . is the parent of Liberty and Ease'), his classical bias made him touchy about the shameless rush to commercialise contemporary writing. Unable to deny such pressures, he tried to preserve a principle of disinterested public service which would transcend any suggestion of self-interest or vanity, vices common to literary as well as to economic speculators.

By 1730, Swift was writing the last of his Irish pamphlets. He wrote six short pieces in 1729, each one responding to a specific issue or person, but decided to publish only one of them, *A Modest Proposal*, at the end of the year. The relationship between the abandoned pamphlets and his most famous one is instructive, as it shows Swift's frustration and horror being rewritten until they find a form of detachment which exercises control of such violent emotion. These 'preliminary' pamphlets, in Ferguson's phrase, lack the 'incendiary appeal' of the earlier tracts,[29] and show a writer almost demented by the absurdity of his efforts to affect the public conscience. The mood which conditioned this attitude is revealed by Swift in a letter to Bolingbroke and Pope, written in April:

> I never wake without finding life a more insignificant thing than it was the day before: which is one great advantage I get by living in this country, where there is nothing I shall be sorry to lose; but my greatest misery is recollecting the scene of twenty years past, and then all on a sudden dropping into the present. I remember when I was a little boy, I felt a great fish at the end of my line which I drew up almost on the ground, but it dropt in, and the disappointment vexeth me to this very day.[30]

Personalised nostalgia of this kind comes as quite a surprise, especially when it occurs in a writer so engaged with contemporary realities. Using the past as a stick to beat the present was both a literary principle as well as an instinctive personal defence. This stance accounts for what F. R. Leavis recognised as Swift's 'negative' power.[31]

One of the first pamphlets of 1729, *A Letter to the Archbishop of Dublin, concerning the Weavers*, shows Swift's efforts to address himself to a specific, local issue, but then being overwhelmed by the magnitude of its implications. Moving from the economic distress of his parishioners to the population at large, he wonders:

... whether those animals which come in my way with two legs and human faces, clad, and erect, be of the same species with what I have seen very like them in England, as to outward Shape, but differing in their notions, natures, and intellectuals more than any two kinds of Brutes in a forest.[32]

This imagery is both a residue of *Gulliver's Travels* and an anticipation of *A Modest Proposal*. The violence of pamphlets like this *Letter* is often directed at female vanity, women becoming an obsessive scapegoat for an insolvent nation. In the *Answer to Several Letters from Unknown Persons*, he rants against women who 'spend the revenue of a moderate family to adorn a nauseous unwholesom living Carcase'.[33] He devoted an entire pamphlet to their responsibilities, *A Proposal to the Ladies of Ireland*, blaming them for the nation's distorted economy. In this stream of puritan outrage, there are moments of coherence, as when he realises that occasional or immediate crises are symptoms not causes:

I will venture to affirm, that the three seasons wherein our corn hath miscarried, did no more contribute to our present misery, than one spoonful of water thrown upon a rat already drowned would contribute to his death.[34]

The lunacy of such superficial gestures captures Swift's problem with writing. Caught between faith and contempt, he ends up talking to himself. Pestered by the letters of so many 'unreasonable well-meaning People', he sees no point in publishing pamphlets to be read by 'half a score people in a Coffee-house'.[35] One such enthusiast was James Maculla, a Dubliner who had proposed a new system of private enterprise in Irish coinage. Reminded of Wood's greed, Swift wrote *A Letter on Maculla's Project*,[36] systematically dismissing Maculla's elaborate and tedious calculations, and classifying the scheme as 'visionary', a key-word in Swift's vocabulary of reform.

Swift's imaginative self-discipline reappeared in *A Modest Proposal*, published in Dublin in late October.[37] All the elements of the year's earlier pamphlets are visible in its design, but now are part of a parodic structure which mocks the pamphlet form itself and those writers, like Swift himself, who claim to be working for national salvation. The nameless proposer of the scheme, whose shocking methods are repeatedly attributed to other, unnamed sources, is well aware of the tradition of reforming pamphleteers. He himself confesses to being 'wearied out for many Years with offering vain, idle, visionary Thoughts', and cleverly substitutes a comprehensive scheme in the place of popular 'Expedients', which turn out to be an inventory of Swift's Irish pamphlets over the previous decade. Coming only five years after the triumph of the Drapier, *A Modest Proposal* shows Swift having written himself out of this kind of literature by an ingenious piece of self-criticism. It would be almost impossible for him to write again with a straight face.

In November 1730, however, exactly a year after what seemed like the definitive anti-pamphlet, he wrote a very similar, and even more extreme, 'solution' to the Irish problem. This was *The Answer to the Craftsman*, a pamphlet provoked by a report in a London journal which exposed the government's secret connivance with French officers who were in Ireland to recruit for foreign service.[38] The political absurdity of such collaboration found expression in the servile persona of Swift's *Answer*, who suggests that, since London seems happy to strip Ireland of her human as well as military resources, she should export the entire population. This would have the immediate advantage of leaving the country empty for grazing cattle and sheep. Like his fictional cousin in *A Modest Proposal*, this persona will stop at nothing to please and serve England. After a decade of intensive pamphleteering, Swift has ended with images of bestiality, murder and desolation. The *Answer* was the last pamphlet Swift wrote on Ireland's material condition.

Writing to Pope in January 1731, Swift described his social and literary routine in classically misanthropic style:

> I am in my Chamber at five, there sit alone till eleven, and then to bed. I write Pamphlets and follys meerly for amusement, and when they are finished, as I grow weary in the middle, I cast them into the fire, partly out of dislike, and chiefly because I know they will signify nothing. I walk much every day and ride once or twice a week and so you have the whole State of my life.[39]

In fact, his social life at this time was quite lively.[40] He neither wrote nor published any pamphlets during the coming year, but he was refining several poetic and prose ventures which would appear over the next decade. He certainly seems to have decided to resist the temptation to engage in personal or political controversies, remarking to a friend, as if to his own surprise, that 'I have not written a libel these six months.'[41] He explained this abstention with ruthless logic – '. . . looking upon this Kingdom's condition as absolutely desperate, I would not prescribe a dose for the dead.'[42] The picture he gave to Pope, of a writer too tired and uninspired to create anything worthwhile, was largely a defensive tactic, since Pope was regularly asking for new material for the next volume of *Miscellanies*. Tracking down copies of his poems and sending them to London for Pope's inspection was a labour which did not suit Swift at the time. Also, such a service tended to diminish Swift's sense of authority and independence: the Dean had other plans for his literary reputation.

Swift's temporary retirement from pamphleteering and his excuses to Pope were a form of camouflage behind which he busied himself with two major essays on social decorum. We first learn of this secretive project in August 1731, when Swift wrote to Gay from Powerscourt, Co. Wicklow, where he was staying with a clerical friend:

> I retired hither for the publick good having two great works in hand, one to reduce the whole politeness, wit, humor & style of England into a short System for the use of all persons of quality, and particularly the Maids of Honor: The other is of almost equal importance; I may call it the whole duty of servants, in about twenty several Stations from the Steward & waiting woman down to the Scullion & Pantry boy.[43]

These 'two great works' turned out to be *Polite Conversation* and *Directions to Servants*, not published until several years later, at that time (1731) undergoing revision and improvement. He soon told Pope about these essays, including the extraordinary fact that he had begun them 'about twenty eight years ago'.[44] He was determined they should be published in London. If we can believe Swift's figure, this would mean he began these works shortly after leaving William Temple's service.

This story confirms a very distinctive pattern in Swift's literary practice, whereby he nursed secret narratives for many years, constantly adding, refining and rewriting. Like *A Tale Of A Tub*, *Gulliver's Travels*, and especially his obsessive *History*, these extended essays were of a very different character from his occasional writings. Swift felt duty-bound to engage with current affairs and passing controversies, but he always kept a place for large-scale works of a more universal kind, works which could be published if and when it suited him. While pamphleteering embodies his Irish dimension, these larger works of patient accumulation reflect the English side of his literary personality.

At the end of 1731, Swift confided to Gay the progress of one of his best-known poems:

> I have been severall months writing near five hundred lines on a pleasant Subject, onely to tell what my friends and enemyes will say on me after I am dead. I shall finish it soon, for I add two lines every week, and blott out four, and alter eight, I have brought in you and my other friends, as well as enemyes and Detractors.[45]

This meticulous writing referred to *Verses on the Death of Dr Swift*, which was not published until 1739, but which was rewritten into a different version and published on April Fool's Day in 1733, with the title *Life and Genuine Character of Dr Swift*.[46] Both poems are based on a maximum from Rochefoucauld, 'In the adversity of our best friends, we find something that doth not displease us'. The *Life* is a shorter account than the *Verses*, and was published without any of the biting political allusions to English politicians which appeared in the later version. Both poems allow Swift to indulge the fantasy of reporting his own death through the mixed responses of friends and enemies, and of eavesdropping on their judgements. The *Life* concludes with the words of a loyal defender of Swift's career:

> 'Tis plain, his writings were designed
> To please, and to reform mankind;
> And, if he often missed his aim,
> The world must own it, to their shame;
> The praise is his, and theirs the blame.
> Then, since you dread no further lashes,
> You freely may forgive his ashes.[47]

Like the conceit behind several of the Markethill poems, the dramatic irony behind these poems is used to give a critical, but tolerant, self-portrait of the writer, someone who was foolish enough to believe the world could be improved. These poems constitute a poetic autobiography ranging over his literary, political and clerical career.

Even though the prospect of his own death afforded Swift a novel form of graveyard humour, the death of friends haunted him during these years. Shortly after the publication of *A Modest Proposal*, he wrote to Bolingbroke: 'I was 47 Years old when I began to think of death; and the reflections upon it now begin when I wake in the Morning, and end when I am going to Sleep.'[48] In that same year, Archbishop King, his loyal superior for fifteen years, had died. Three years later, in December 1732, one of his best-loved literary friends, John Gay, died. Swift's literary career was now drawing to a close.

7

A Poetic Valediction

During the last decade of his literary career, Swift's public writing was dominated by local and immediate issues of Church and State.[1] The material well-being of the Irish clergy and the legal toleration of religious Dissent reappeared as controversial topics in a series of pamphlets published during the years 1732–3, and showed Swift's stubborn defence of lifelong fundamentalist principles about the rights of the Established Church and the potential subversiveness of all other creeds. He even reprinted his 1708 pamphlet on the Test, a striking mark of inflexible consistency on these questions. Most of the pamphlets reiterate a familiar orthodoxy in forceful, if predictable, language. Yet Swift's conservatism also defends the lower, not the ruling, clergy: this often gives his intransigent message a liberal character. In *A Proposal to Pay Off the Debt of the Nation*, published by Faulkner in March 1732, he adopts the mask of a 'perfect Stranger' to Ireland, and offers an elaborate scheme whereby the propertied wealth of the bishops would, in true Christian fashion, be willingly sold off for the benefit of the country. This ironic use of a mask, once a standard feature of Swift's pamphlets, is by now exceptional, since most of his writings on these issues are without any attempt at humour or disguise. Although he continued to withhold his signature, he spoke in his own voice.

Because of old age and recurrent illness, Swift now rarely ventured out of Dublin. This enforced residence drew him into the civic and municipal affairs of the capital more closely than ever before. He took an active interest in the political administration of the city, knowing many of its figures personally and socially. His attenuated commitment to public reform now switched from national to parochial issues, in a dwindling series of plaintive, often eccentric, proposals. On two occasions when candidates stood for public office, he wrote and published pamphlets explaining and defending the merits of his choice. These were *Considerations in the Choice of a Recorder* and *Advice to the Freemen of Dublin*, which appeared in the summer of 1733, both unsigned but clearly inspired by the Drapier's kind of practical patriotism.[2] Despite Swift's cultural self-image as an Englishman in exile, two decades of living and writing in Ireland had clearly affected his sense of political loyalty. As one of the most eloquent spokesmen for the colonial interest in Ireland, Swift could now articulate a changed sense of identity, born out of bitter experience. In *Advice to the Freemen of Dublin*, in which he urged people to ignore the government's candidate for a vacant seat in parliament, and to support a local patriot, he wrote:

> ... the great Men in Power sent hither from the other Side were by no means upon the same Foot with his Majesty's other Subjects of *Ireland*. They had no common Ligament to bind them with us; they suffered not with our Sufferings, and if it were possible for us to have any Cause of Rejoycing, they could not rejoyce with us.[3]

With an irony he could never acknowledge, the anglophile Dean had done more than anyone else to encourage this sense of isolation and abandonment. As a writer, Swift had reflected and shaped an emergent political consciousness in Protestant Ireland which was loyal but defiant, separate but dependent. When he spoke, his people listened: in the election, his recommended candidate won the seat.[4]

In the other miscellaneous pamphlets written by Swift in these years, there is little that is new or inspired. His endless obsession with money and inflation provoked him into print on a couple of occasions,[5] and he would sometimes write a short 'Answer' to a pamphlet sent to him by some enthusiastic reformer.[6] One of his more bizarre, but not uncharacteristic, productions was *A Proposal for Giving Badges to Beggars*, written and published in April 1737, when he was nearly seventy. In almost the same tones of civilised outrage and pity used by the projector of *A Modest Proposal*, but here without the slightest irony, Swift contemplates the scandalous problem of Dublin's mendicant poor and, with his usual love of regimentation, proposes the strictest municipal supervision of these beggars, blaming their inherent wickedness for their disgusting condition. This should be, but is not, parody. The desperate scheme ends with a familiar complaint: '... it will be thought, that I have already said too much, and to little or no Purpose; which hath often been the Fate, or Fortune of the Writer.'[7] Then, most unusually, comes his signature. This cranky but coherent piece was the last pamphlet ever written by Swift.

During these final years, Swift's poetry shows much greater energy and originality than his prose. He produced a series of daring parodies of romantic love, now termed his 'scatalogical' or 'excremental' verse.[8] The first of these, *The Lady's Dressing Room*, was published in 1732 by J. Roberts in London, along with some Markethill verse.[9] In this kind of poetry, Swift combined his love of parody with a talent for shocking detail and dramatic characterisation, all in the service of a realistic view of female beauty. When the poet, with voyeuristic passion, shows the artifice behind the image of femininity, he both entertains and disturbs the reader. His purpose is to show how the physical and the spiritual, the material and the ideal, are related in ways which could disappoint only the naive and the sentimental. Poor Strephon, the ardent lover, has to accept the 'lower' nature of his darling Celia, and then:

> He soon would learn to think like me,
> And bless his ravished Sight to see
> Such Order from Confusion sprung,
> Such gaudy Tulips rais'd from Dung.[10]

The explicit obscenity of some of the verse had to be justified as part of a moral intent, and Swift took pains to write and publish an anonymous *Defence* of his poem.[11] In it he rejects charges of perversity or morbidity, emphasising the 'useful Satyr running through every Line, and the Matter as decently wrapp'd up, as it is possible the Subject could bear.' He also uses the tactic of classical precedent to his own advantage, arguing that his lines on this delicate subject are the epitome of decency and reserve when compared with those by Horace. The 'Hibernian Bard', as he puts it, wins the laurel for stylistic discretion.

Two years later, in December 1734, Swift arranged for Roberts to publish a quarto pamphlet containing three similar poems. These new variations on the scatalogical theme were *A Beautiful Young Nymph Going to Bed*, *Strephon and Chloe*, and *Cassinus and Peter*, all written, as the title says, 'for the Honour of the Fair Sex'.[12] It should be remembered, of course, that Swift had written verse like this before, such as *The Progress of Beauty* (1720), a poem which Stella had copied out for him. Ehrenpreis rightly emphasises the importance of Swift's platonic relationship with Stella and Vanessa when considering these anti-feminine poems.[13] In *Strephon and Chloe*, the poet mocks the young lovers' foolish obsession with passing, sensual pleasures:

> But, e'er you sell your self to Laughter,
> Consider well what may come after;
> For fine Ideas vanish fast,
> While all the gross and filthy last.[14]

In a most conventional ending to a most radical poem, Swift soberly recommends intellectual and emotional friendship as the most enduring love of all.

As well as seeing these poems as ironic compliments to the memory of Stella and the 'masculine' woman, or as evidence of Swift's misogyny, we might also recognise their place in his writings on decorum and manners. Their violent and obscene imagery, as in pamphlets like *A Modest Proposal*, is central to Swift's war on a class of civilised people who often behave like animals. As part of a corrective parody, Swift also mocks those romantic poets who deny the mortality of women. Courtly romance is reduced, through farcical circumstance, to a recognition of its lower nature. Having spent a great deal of his life amongst the upper classes of both England and Ireland, Swift took an almost sadistic pleasure in deflating their pretensions.

In the middle of this decade, Swift wrote his last major poem, *A Character, Panegyric, and Description of the Legion Club*, a work which shows undiminished ferocity in its defence of the Church and in its loathing for all those who pretend to care for its survival.[15] In the spring of 1736, the Irish parliament had voted to remove certain tithes from the Church, an action which enraged the Dean, always hyper-sensitive about clerical finances. Accordingly, he dubbed this blasphemous parliament 'Legion', to suggest its infernal and diabolical nature. In April, writing to Sheridan, he told his friend, 'I have wrote a very masterly Poem on the Legion-Club,' which he was planning to publish in London, since the references to Irish MPs made it too dangerous for Dublin. It appeared in June, as part of a small miscellany, and was only printed in Dublin after Swift's death. Full of personal invective and abuse, written in lively, blunt couplets, *The Legion Club* is remarkably energetic and coherent as the work of a poet almost seventy years of age. It employs a vulgarity of manner deserved by its subject:

> Let them, when they once get in
> Sell the Nation for a Pin;
> While they sit a picking Straws
> Let them rave of making Laws;
> While they never hold their Tongue,
> Let them dabble in their Dung;
> Let them for a grand Committee,
> How to plague and starve the City;
> Let them stare and storm and frown,
> When they see a Clergy-Gown.
> Let them, 'ere they crack a Louse,
> Call for th'Orders of the House;
> Let them with their gosling Quills,
> Scribble senseless Heads of Bills;
> We may, while they strain their Throats,
> Wipe our A---s with their V----.[16]

Invoking the inspiration of the London cartoonist, Hogarth, he pictures the Dublin parliament as a Bedlam inhabited by vicious and noisome animals, incapable of logical argument or imaginative vision. Like the fallen world behind *Gulliver's Travels*, the barbarism of *A Modest Proposal*, or the sheer lunacy in *A Tale Of A Tub*, this poem's image of hell creates a fantasy of distortion suited to the horror of the occasion. *The Legion Club* shows, in spectacular fashion, that Swift did not mellow with age. He forgot and forgave nothing.

After 1736, Swift virtually ceased writing imaginative work in prose or verse, although he wrote letters until his last moments of rationality and competence. However, he still wanted to dispose of those lengthy compositions which he had nurtured for years. These were now delegated to friends who, on Swift's instructions, arranged for publication in London. The satirical *Polite Conversation* was one of several manuscripts carried over to England in 1738 by Lord Orrery. Published by Motte the following year, this 'Collection of Genteel and Ingenious Conversation' was a characteristic subject for Swift, but this time rendered in the unusual form of extended dramatic dialogues. Begun in the reign of Queen Anne, it is a series of three conversations held by the members and friends of a courtly family resident in London. The company is wealthy but witless, a characteristic of that class often noted by Swift. While the dialogues are an amusing collection of platitudes, clichés, proverbs, slang and barbarisms, showing the inane mentality of the gentry, the 'Introduction' by Simon Wagstaff is the funniest element of the entire travesty. Here Swift impersonates the type he most despises, a fashionable toady. Wagstaff is the last of Swift's idiotic projectors, full of self-importance and bereft of taste, now offering his collection of fashionable conversation as a model for practising 'wit'. Proud of his ignorance of 'useless' learning, and flattered by his political contacts at Court, he mocks the reputed 'talents' of the age: 'Let the Popes, the Gays, the Arbuthnots, the Youngs, and the rest of that snarling Brood, burst with Envy at the Praises we receive from the Court and Kingdom.'[17] The character of Wagstaff, embellished over many years, is one of Swift's funniest works of rhetorical irony. The dialogues which he introduces – the closest thing to a play which Swift ever wrote – are clever but mechanical. Swift's talent lay with character not drama.

The same point may be made about *Directions to Servants*, a companion-piece to *Polite Conversation*. It is like a manual or catechism of behaviour proper to an extensive range of servants, which combines Swift's love of order and propriety. That the text has survived in print is a small miracle since, as late as 1739, Swift was writing to his Dublin publisher, George Faulkner, asking him to help find most of the manuscript, saying, 'I wish you could give me some Intelligence of it, because, my Memory is quite gone.'[18] In May 1740, Mrs Whiteway wrote to Pope, telling him that the papers had been found, but that Swift was now too ill to correct or finish them.[19] The *Directions to Servants* was finally published in London and Dublin in November 1745, a month after Swift's death.

Like *Polite Conversation*, the *Directions* belong to Swift's extensive writings on social decorum. It is noteworthy, however, that a satirical manner is reserved for the ignorance of the upper classes while an earnest appeal is made to the intelligence of their inferiors. Nothing seems funnier or more outrageous than the follies of civilised man: nothing is more serious than the smooth machinery of service. Swift's attitude is a curious mixture of respect and contempt, an attitude never employed exclusively for one particular class. Inexcusable ignorance was to be found amongst countesses as well as cooks. His *Directions* are, like his sermons, an appeal for orderly and responsible behaviour. Swift knew quite a lot about servants, both from experience and observation: he began his literary career as the servant to a gentleman, and his country of birth was a servant to his country of ambition.

While Swift continued to send some important individual pieces to London, he was privately negotiating an authoritative Dublin edition of his entire literary canon. His experience with the *Miscellanies* and the editions of *Gulliver's Travels* seems to have made him accept the obvious and practical advantage of supervising an edition in Dublin. This turned out to be the most significant decision of Swift's last years. He had always been unable or unwilling to consider Dublin as a city worthy of literary distinction: 'literature' meant London. But now his values had altered, and a strong competitive loyalty to Ireland had emerged. Swift entrusted his work and reputation to George Faulkner, the 'Prince of Dublin Printers'.[20]

The problem was how to maintain the friendship with Pope, and the business relationship with Motte. Swift had promised both the poet and the publisher legal control of his work, but only after his death.[21] Early in 1733, Faulkner started advertising the projected edition in his own newspaper, the *Dublin Journal*, while Swift quickly wrote to Pope denying any support for such an idea.[22] But at the end of the year, Swift wrote to Charles Ford, making it clear that a supervised Dublin edition would ensure a more correct and authentic version of his work than Motte, Pope and others had achieved.[23] He was especially concerned about 'that mingled and mangled manner' of his *Travels*. Ford approved and encouraged Swift's plan:

> I have long had it at heart to see your works collected, and published with care. It is become absolutely necessary, since that jumble with Pope &c. in three volumes, which put me in a rage whenever I meet them.[24]

Ford drew up a list of pieces written by Swift, of which he held copies, and promised to send them to Dublin if the originals were lost. Although Swift never once voiced direct approval of Faulkner's project, and continued to protest his unwilling and passive involvement, it is inconceivable that he did not give first-hand advice to Faulkner, who had worked loyally for the Dean since first publishing some of the Drapier's *Letters* nearly ten years previously. Faulkner himself later testified to the Dean's very close involvement in preparing the edition.[25]

Faulkner's first edition of Swift's *Works*, published by subscription, appeared in January 1735. Only a few weeks after this historic event in his career, Swift wrote to William Pulteney disowning the edition, 'done utterly against my will', and professing a certain embarrassment that it should appear 'in so obscure a place'.[26] Swift's real feelings on the issue were forced out into the open by Motte's indignation at the prospect of an Irish publisher ready to exploit the London market. In July, he wrote to Swift, asking for sympathy and support, and then threatened a legal injunction against Faulkner's edition.[27] Motte persisted in his complaints and demands until Swift exploded with politicised anger:

> ... only one Thing I know, that the cruel Oppressions of this Kingdom by England are not to be borne. You send what Books you please hither, and the Book-sellers here can send nothing to you that is written here ... Mr Faulkner hath dealt so fairly with me, that I have a great Opinion of his Honesty ...[28]

Swift now saw this dispute over copyright in terms of those constitutional liberties he had defended as the Drapier, with Motte and Co. now playing the villain's role. Despite this legal wrangle, Faulkner continued with his Dublin edition, adding three more volumes before Swift died.[29] Thereafter, for over twenty years he gathered manuscripts until, in 1769, he was able to present a completed set of twenty volumes of Swift's writings.[30] Precisely because of Swift's original assistance, Faulkner has remained the most authoritative text.

Those who could make legal claim to Swift's writings, either with or without the author's consent, would enjoy financial reward as well as a share in the Dean's immortality. Because manuscript copies of much of his work were scattered among the houses of friends in England and Ireland, and because he could no longer even remember where certain manuscripts were, Swift's literary estate became a very desirable, but elusive, property. This was especially true of his private correspondence.

Pope, whose own *Works* began to appear in April 1735, planned to bring out an edition of the letters between himself and Swift. Hearing nothing but reports of his friend's declining health, and not wishing to appear like a literary grave-robber, he used a mutual friend, Lord Orrery, to persuade the Dean to release any letters in his possession. Swift's response, in September, aggravated Pope's difficult position, telling him that legal executors 'have strict orders

in my will to burn every letter left behind me'.[31] He tells Pope, not
for the first time, that he views their letters, not as works of literary
significance or value, but as 'mere innocent friendship'. Swift's
attitude to the value of such a correspondence is less teasing and
more open in a letter he wrote to Lady Germain only a few months
before that to Pope:

> . . . I never burn a letter that is entertaining, and consequently
> will give me new pleasure when it is forgotten. It is true, I have
> kept some letters merely out of friendship, although they
> sometimes wanted true spelling and good sense, and some
> others whose writers are dead. For I live like a monk, and hate to
> forget my departed friends.[32]

The hunt for his original letters to Swift took several years for Pope
to conclude. Swift himself seemed at first quite wary, even
disapproving, but eventually he complied. In June 1737, Swift
entrusted about twenty-five letters to Orrery (along with the
manuscript of *Polite Conversation*), and asked him to deliver them to
Pope while passing through London.[33] In May 1740, after three
years of intrigue and deception worthy of the Dean himself, Pope
sent Swift a printed copy of their correspondence, swearing it was
the only copy in existence, specially produced to celebrate their
friendship.[34] A year later, in April 1741, Pope reproduced this
correspondence in the second volume of his *Prose Works*. As editor,
he deleted all his own requests to Swift for the return of his
letters.[35] In June of the same year, Faulkner reprinted this edition
of the correspondence as the seventh volume of his edition of
Swift's *Works*.

However genuine and deep the friendship between Swift and
Pope, the fact that it had been conducted for so long through
letters alone, gave it a remote and stylised character. At another
extreme is Swift's friendship with Sheridan, which always brought
out Swift's humour. Only once in the last fifteen years of his life
did he venture outside the city, when he spent a final holiday with
Sheridan in Cavan during the winter of 1735, after repeated and
playful invitations from the scholarly teacher. In a joint letter to
Mrs Whiteway, the two clergymen sound like boys absconded
from school: their talk is of wine and food, horseriding, riddles and
puns, wet turf and hopeless servants.[36] Sheridan, whom Swift
described as 'the most learned Person I know in this Kingdom',

died three years later. Other friends died during this decade, Arbuthnot in 1735, and Lady Acheson in 1737. In a letter to John Barber, Swift wrote, 'What a havoc hath death made among our friends since that of the Queen!'[37] Swift, the hypochondriac, was outliving most of his contemporaries.

At the end of the decade, Swift wrote his will, a document generous in spirit, severe in style.[38] On 26 July 1740, he wrote to Mrs Whiteway:

> I have been very miserable all night, and today extremely deaf and full of pain. I am so stupid and confounded, that I cannot express the mortification I am under both in body and mind. All I can say is, that I am not in torture; but I daily and hourly expect it. Pray let me know how your health is, and your family. I hardly understand one word I write. I am sure my days will be very few; few and miserable they must be.[39]

This was the last personal letter he wrote. Despite his painful certainties, he lived for five more years, most of the time under the care of appointed guardians.

There is an anecdotal tale about Swift's last literary composition, a story relayed by one of those guardians. Out for a walk in the Phoenix Park in Dublin, Swift noticed a new, military fortification, and asked his accompanying doctor about its purpose. Being told that it was built to defend the city, Swift laughed, and made a note in a pocket-book he carried. The incident resulted in a final epigram:

> Behold! a proof of Irish sense!
> Here Irish wit is seen!
> When nothing's left that's worth defence,
> We build a magazine.[40]

The literary career of this outstanding prose satirist, lasting half a century, began and ended with verse. Swift died on 19 October 1745, aged seventy-eight.

Notes

PW refers to H. Davis, ed., *The Prose Works of Jonathan Swift*, 14 vols (Oxford, 1939–68), and H. Williams, ed., *The Journal to Stella*, 2 vols (Oxford, 1948). *Poems* refers to H. Williams, ed., *The Poems of Jonathan Swift*, 3 vols, 2nd edn rev. (Oxford, 1958). *Corr* refers to H. Williams, ed., *The Correspondence of Jonathan Swift*, 5 vols (Oxford, 1963–5, vols IV and V partially revised by D. Woolley, 1972).

Chapter 1

1. The most detailed, scholarly account of Swift's family background may be found in Irvin Ehrenpreis, *Swift: The Man, His Works, and The Age*, 3 vols (London, 1962–83) I, *Mr Swift and his Contemporaries* pp. 3–7. For Swift's own version of his ancestry, an incomplete fragment of autobiography, see *PW*, V, pp. 187–92.
2. *PW*, V, pp. 188–9.
3. Ibid., p. 192.
4. See Ehrenpreis, I, pp. 34–42.
5. *PW*, V, p. 192.
6. *Corr*, I, pp. 1–2.
7. For a detailed biographical and stylistic discussion of these poems see Ehrenpreis, I, pp. 109–41.
8. *Poems*, I, pp. 17–18.
9. *Corr*, I, p. 4.
10. Ibid., p. 8.
11. Ibid., p. 9. Williams notes that Swift kept an annotated copy of Cowley's verse in his library all his life.
12. *Poems*, I, p. 40.
13. Ehrenpreis, I, p. 141.
14. *Corr*, I, p. 12.
15. It was, however, finally enacted in 1694.
16. *PW*, V, p. 194.
17. *Corr*, I, p. 16. Swift even asked this cousin (a son of Uncle Godwin), who had settled in Portugal with a trading mission, if he could find him a chaplaincy in Lisbon.
18. *PW*, V, p. 194.
19. *Corr*, I, pp. 16–17.
20. Ibid., p. 17.
21. See L. Landa, *Swift and the Church of Ireland* (Oxford, 1965) pp. 10–24.
22. *Corr*, I, pp. 18–23.
23. The most comprehensive analysis of this issue is found in *A Tale Of A Tub*, edited by A. C. Guthkelch and D. Nichol Smith, 2nd edn (Oxford, 1958) pp. xliii–xlvii. This is now widely regarded as an authoritative edition of the *Tale*, and all subsequent references are to this text. See also *PW*, I, pp. xv–xvi and Ehrenpreis, I, p. 187.

24. See *PW*, I, p. 9.
25. See Ehrenpreis, I, p. 186 and p. 195.
26. *Tale*, pp. xvii–xviii.
27. *Corr*, I, pp. 165–6.
28. Ibid., p. 27.
29. Ibid., p. 31.
30. Williams, in his Introduction to the *Correspondence*, points out that, unlike Alexander Pope, Swift 'exhibited no desire to see his letters in print'. On the sermons, see L. Landa's 'Introduction' in *PW*, IX, pp. 97–8, which confirms this seeming indifference to the literary fate of the sermons.
31. *PW*, I, p. 258.
32. Most of this detail is from Ehrenpreis, I, p. 260.
33. *Corr*, I, p. 39.
34. *Tale*, p. 5.
35. Ibid., p. 131. The editors note that Dryden's Dedication to *Juvenal* ran to fifty-three pages, and that to *Aeneis* forty-seven pages.
36. Ibid., pp. 207–8.
37. See Introduction to the *Tale*, pp. xxii–xxv. Wotton's *Observations* and Curll's *Complete Key* are reprinted in the Appendices, pp. 313–48.
38. See Ehrenpreis, I, pp. 179–82. This discussion centres almost exclusively on epistolary style.
39. *Tale*, p. 240.
40. See Ehrenpreis' discussion of the significance of this imagery, in Ehrenpreis, I, p. 244ff, in which he rejects the controversial interpretation, based on Freud, put forward by Norman O. Brown in his *Life Against Death* (London, 1959).
41. *Tale*, pp. 288–9.
42. See Introduction to the *Tale*, pp. lv–lx, where a list of Swift's reading for the year 1697–8 is reproduced. This list was originally printed in Sheridan's *Life of Swift* (1784), from one of Swift's early memoranda.
43. *PW*, I, p. xxiii.
44. See Introduction to the *Tale*, pp. lxv–lxxvii.

Chapter 2

1. *Corr*, I, pp. 44–5.
2. *PW*, I, p. xxxiv.
3. *Corr*, I, p. 54.
4. *PW*, I, pp. 241–5.
5. Ibid.
6. In the *Miscellanies*. The *Meditation*, however, was printed separately by Edmund Curll in 1710, having 'obtained' a copy from his lodger. See *PW*, I, p. 302. Curll was clearly interested in Swift's work, and published a *Key* to the *Tale* in the same year. In 1711 he brought out a pirated edition of the *Miscellanies*. All of this, of course, without Swift's consent.
7. *PW*, IX, p. 3.
8. See Irvin Ehrenpreis, *Swift: The Man, His Works, and The Age*, II, Dr

Swift, pp. 230–51 for a very detailed and lively discussion of this literary circle.

9. *PW*, II, p. 145.
10. See Davis' 'Introduction', ibid., pp. x–xiv.
11. Ibid., p. xiv.
12. Ibid., pp. xxv–xxviii.
13. *Corr*, I, pp. 84–7.
14. *PW*, II, pp. xix–xx.
15. *Corr*, I, p. 100.
16. *PW*, II, p. 2.
17. Ibid., p. 10.
18. Ibid., p. 36.
19. Ibid., p. 32.
20. Ehrenpreis, II, p. 277ff.
21. This list is reproduced in Ehrenpreis, II, Appendix B, pp. 768–9.
22. *PW*, II, p. 56.
23. To Robert Hunter, *Corr*, I, p. 133.
24. This was *Tatler*, no. 4, 18 April. See *PW*, II, p. xxvii.
25. See Ehrenpreis, II, pp. 301–2. He makes an interesting classification of literary types, comparing Swift to Johnson and Bunyan, and contrasting them with writers like Temple, Gray and Walpole whose aesthetic was never limited to literature alone.
26. *Corr*, I, p. 139.
27. See Davis' 'Introduction', in *PW*, II, pp. xxi–xxii.
28. *PW*, II, p. 114.
29. Ibid., p. 120.
30. *Corr*, I, p. 125.
31. Ibid., p. 126.
32. Ibid., p. 134.
33. *Poems*, I, pp. 124–5.

Chapter 3

1. Sheridan, in his edition of 1784, called the collection *Dr Swift's Journal to Stella*, and John Nichols, in 1779, gave it its present title. See *PW*, XV, p. 1.
2. In 1776, John Hawkesworth edited and published twenty-six letters, numbers 1 and 41 to 65, the originals of which still survive. In 1778, Deane Swift edited and published thirty-nine other letters. None of the originals of these later letters survive. Most of the *Journal*, therefore, is based on Deane Swift's edition, which is not always thought reliable. See Williams' 'Introduction', *PW*, XV, pp. xlvii–lix for details of various editions.
3. Two distinguished exceptions are I. Ehrenpreis, 'Swift's Letters', in *Swift*, ed. C. J. Rawson (London, 1971) pp. 197–215, and D. Wooley, 'Talkative on Paper', *Classics*, 6 May 1968, pp. 2–4.
4. Although Swift must have been tempted, since he took care to preserve them. In March 1713, towards the end of the *Journal*, he acknowledged their unique value by remarking, 'My letters would

be good Memoirs if I durst say a thousd things that pass.' See *PW*, XVI, p. 638.

5.   *PW*, XV, p. 167.
6.   Ibid., p. 210.
7.   Ibid., p. 342.
8.   Ibid., p. 414.
9.   *PW*, II, p. 174.
10. *Poems*, I, p. 137.
11. When the poem was reprinted the following year in the *Miscellanies*, Swift added a footnote to these lines, explaining why Dryden and other poets in the reign of Charles II introduced these variations. He stated that they were the result of 'Haste, Idleness and want of Money'! See *Poems*, I, p. 139.
12. *PW*, XV, p. 63.
13. Ibid., p. 36.
14. See Irvin Ehrenpreis, *Swift: The Man, His Works, and The Age*, II, *Dr Swift*, pp. 406–22 for incisive discussion. The whole volume is one of the most eloquent and comprehensive accounts of this period in Swift's writing career. See also Michael Foot's *The Pen and the Sword* (London, 1957) and J. Downie's *Jonathan Swift: Political Writer* (London, 1984).
15. *PW*, III, p. 149.
16. Ibid., p. 147.
17. Ibid., pp. 171–2.
18. On Marlborough, see especially 'To Crassus', no. 27. On Wharton, see the notorious 'The Art of Political Lying', no. 14, and an anonymous pamphlet *A Short Character of his Excellency Thomas Earl of Wharton*, published in December 1710. Swift mentions this 'libellous pamphlet' to Stella, approving its style but not its facts, wondering mischievously who the author might be. See *PW*, III, pp. 231–40, and *PW*, XV, p. 115.
19. *PW*, III, p. 36.
20. Ibid., pp. 76–7.
21. *PW*, XV, p. 108.
22. Ibid., p. 291.
23. *Corr*, I, p. 166. Swift's usage of book trade terms can be misleading for modern readers. By 'publisher', as here with Steele, he means 'editor', by 'bookseller' he means 'publisher'.
24. *PW*, XV, p. 203.
25. Ibid., p. 128.
26. Ibid., p. 294.
27. Ibid., p. 349.
28. Ibid., p. 358.
29. Ibid., p. 343.
30. *PW*, XVI, p. 408.
31. The following are Swift's own details. *PW*, XVI, pp. 427–8.
32. A point emphasised in Ehrenpreis, II, p. 485ff.
33. *PW*, XVI, pp. 439–40.
34. *PW*, XV, p. 276.

35. Ibid., pp. 474–5.
36. Ehrenpreis is quick to point out the irony of Swift's eagerness to share Harley's fame, since the politician now lives on in Swift's footnotes. Ehrenpreis, II, pp. 548–9.
37. *PW*, IV, p. 20.
38. See Davis, ibid., pp. xiii–xiv.
39. John Toland, the deist author of *The Grand Mystery laid open* (London, 1714), later attacked Swift as a Tory hack, singling out this *Proposal* as evidence of his slavishness. See *PW*, IV, p. xiv.
40. *PW*, XVI, p. 556.
41. Ibid., p. 556.
42. Ibid., p. 569.
43. Ibid., p. 598.
44. Ibid., p. 602.
45. Ibid., p. 654.
46. See *Corr*, III, p. 31, and V, p. 246, for Swift's views on Berkeley.
47. *PW*, XVI, p. 662.
48. Ehrenpreis, II, pp. 632–3.
49. Ehrenpreis, II, p. 646, in a skilful piece of detective-work, compares entries in Swift's account-books with the *Journal*, and points to evenings spent with the Vanhomrighs which become 'meetings with my printer' in letters to Stella.
50. A near-identical conceit is used by the Gaelic poet, Brian Merriman, in his burlesque *Cúirt an Mhean Oíche* (*The Midnight Court*), written at the end of the eighteenth century. Merriman's hilarious poem is often described in 'Swiftian' terms. See Vivian Mercier, *The Irish Comic Tradition* (Oxford, 1962) pp. 194–5.
51. *Poems*, II, p. 703.
52. *Corr*, I, p. 373.
53. *Poems*, I, pp. 171–2.
54. In fact, Steele had written three plays by then, *The Funeral* (1701), *The Lying Lover* (1704) and *The Tender Husband* (1705), sentimental farces which met with little success. After the fall of the Tories, however, he was appointed Governor of Drury Lane.
55. *PW*, VIII, pp. 5–6.
56. Ibid., p. 32.
57. Ibid., p. 43.
58. A point often made by Ehrenpreis, usefully reminding us of the variety of styles excluded or denied by the stereotype of a 'satirical genius'.
59. *Corr*, I, p. 415.
60. *Poems*, I, pp. 193–4.
61. 'Horace, Lib. 2. Sar. 6.', ibid., p. 202.
62. *PW*, VIII, p. 96.
63. See *Corr*, II, pp. 43–4 for Swift's instruction to Ford; for Ford's report to Swift on the progress of the scheme, see ibid., pp. 50–1.
64. *PW*, VIII, p. 200.

Chapter 4

1. *Poems*, I, p. 203.
2. *Corr*, II, pp. 126–7.
3. Ibid., p. 168.
4. Ibid., p. 176.
5. Ibid., p. 465.
6. Ibid., p. 215.
7. By Harold Williams, *Corr*, II, p. 215, n.4.
8. Prior never lived to benefit from this project. He died soon after the work was published, aged fifty-eight.
9. *Corr*, II, p. 333–4.
10. The original copy of this catalogue was in the possession of Mr T. P. Le Fanu, who read his analysis of the document to the Royal Irish Academy in April 1927. See 'Catalogue of Dean Swift's Library in 1715, with an Inventory of his personal property in 1742', *PRIA*, 1927, vol. XXXVII, pp. 262–73. A few years later, Harold Williams published a short book, complementing and extending Le Fanu's paper, on the strength of a hitherto unknown manuscript copy of the 1742 sale catalogue of Swift's library, drawn up when the aged Dean was terminally ill. This catalogue was used by the printer, Faulkner, to advertise the public auction of the library in 1746, the year after Swift's death. Most, but not all, of the books in the 1715 catalogue reappear in the 1742 list. See Williams' *Dean Swift's Library* (Cambridge, 1932). The following discussion is indebted to these two valuable sources.
11. Quoted in *Dean Swift's Library*, p. 22.
12. Delaney published his *Observations upon Lord Orrery's Remarks* in 1754, and a *Life of Swift* was published by the young Sheridan in 1784.
13. *Poems*, III, p. 984.
14. *Corr*, II, p. 301.
15. *Poems*, I, pp. 215–16.
16. Esther Johnson was born on 13 March 1681 in Richmond, Surrey. For details about her family and dates of early meetings with Swift, see *PW*, XV, p. xxiv.
17. *Poems*, II, pp. 721–2.
18. Herbert Davis suggests the name 'Stella' is Swift's contrasting allusion to Philip Sidney's 'Astrophel and Stella'. See his *Stella: A Gentlewoman of the Eighteenth Century* (New York, 1942) p. 12.
19. *Poems*, II, p. 726.
20. Ibid., p. 729.
21. *Corr*, II, p. 326.
22. *Poems*, I, p. 226.
23. In a short essay, *A Letter to a Young Lady*, written in 1723, Swift outlined his general views and prescriptions on female behaviour. In an argument which defies any simplistic characterisation of him as manic mysoginist, he recommends an intellectual woman who deserves to be taken seriously. See *PW*, IX, pp. 85–94.

24. See Ehrenpreis's interesting discussion of Swift's contribution to this well-established genre, in his *Swift: The Man, His Works, and The Age*, III, *Dean Swift*, pp. 103–7. Prior had written several pieces of this kind in his own *Poems*.

25. For the authoritative account of Swift's commitment to his new duties, see Louis Landa, *Swift and the Church of Ireland* (Oxford, 1965) pp. 68–95.

26. *Corr*, II, p. 155.

27. As far back as Kilroot, he had told his successor, Rev. John Winder, to burn any sermons left behind. For a detailed introduction to Swift's sermons see L. Landa, *PW*, IX, pp. 97–137. For a rare look at how Swift worked on the text of a sermon, see H. Davis, 'The Manuscript of Swift's Sermon on Brotherly Love', in J. L. Clifford and L. A. Landa (eds) *Pope and his Contemporaries* (Oxford, 1949) pp. 147–58.

28. *PW*, IX, p. 174.

29. For vivid historical and social accounts of Swift's parish, see Maurice Craig, *Dublin 1660–1860* (Dublin, 1980) pp. 88–93, and Patrick Fagan, *The Second City: Portrait of Dublin 1700–1760* (Dublin, 1986) pp. 223–33.

30. *PW*, IX, p. 72.

31. Ibid., p. 77.

32. Ibid., p. 66.

33. In the 1735 edition of his *Works*, Swift placed this *Letter* immediately after the *Proposal* to Oxford. See *PW*, IX, p. xxiv.

34. *Corr*, II, p. 330.

35. See J. G. Simms, *Colonial Nationalism, 1698–1776* (Cork, 1976), for an historical analysis of these constitutional issues, especially pp. 10–50.

36. *Corr*, II, p. 342.

37. See O. Ferguson, *Jonathan Swift and Ireland* (Urbana, Illinois, 1962) p. 53ff., for details of other, mostly anonymous pamphlets protesting against the Declaratory Act. One of these, *Hibernia's Passive Obedience*, printed by Edmund Waters (who published Swift's 1720 *Proposal*), contained extracts from early writings by Swift on the Irish question, such as *Letter Concerning the Sacramental Test*. This suggests that the Dean's reputation was well established in Ireland. Ferguson's excellent study, amazingly, is the only book-length account of Swift's Irish pamphlets.

38. *PW*, IX, p. 17.

39. Ibid., p. 18. The allusion is to Ecclesiastes 7.7.

40. This *Letter*, never intended to be sent to Pope, may be read in either *Corr*, II, pp. 365–74 or *PW*, IX, pp. 25–34. For the complicated history of its eventual publication see Davis, *PW*, IX, p. xii.

41. *PW*, IX, p. 33.

42. Ibid., p. 34.

43. Ehrenpreis, III, p. 162.

44. For fuller detail, see Ferguson, *Jonathan Swift and Ireland*, pp. 60–2.

45. Editors disagree on the extent of Swift's responsibility for some of

the Bank pamphlets. See *PW*, IX, pp. xvii–xxii. Swift's companion in such pranks, Sheridan, seems to have written several in the same style.

46. *PW*, IX, p. 287.
47. *Corr*, II, pp. 411–12.
48. *Poems*, I, p. 275.
49. Exact population figures for this period are still controversial, but a degree of consensus suggests that Dublin's population was around 140,000 inhabitants, while the country as a whole contained somewhere between three and four million people. See Fagan, *The Second City*, pp. 10–12.
50. *Poems*, I, p. 244. Many of the bibliographical details of this section are based on Williams' commentary.
51. *Corr*, I, p. 381. This is taken to be Swift's first allusion to the composition of his famous satire.
52. *Corr*, II, p. 428.
53. Some fascinating answers to this question may be read in C. Fabricant, *Swift's Landscape* (Baltimore and London, 1982) pp. 62–3, 81–2, 95–6.
54. *PW*, IX, p. 21.
55. In her will, Vanessa left half her money to the young George Berkeley, who declared he hardly knew his benefactor. She left nothing to Swift. See Ehrenpreis, III, pp. 389–90.
56. See *Poems*, I, pp. 315–19 for text and English translation by William Durkin.

Chapter 5

1. The most authoritative literary–historical accounts of the Wood's halfpence controversy and Swift's role as Drapier may be found in Ferguson, *Jonathan Swift and Ireland*, pp. 83–138, and Irvin Ehrenpreis, *Swift: The Man, His Works, and The Age*, III, *Dean Swift*, pp. 187–318. See also J. M. Treadwell, 'Swift, William Wood, and the Factual Basis of Satire', *Journal of British Studies*, XV, no. 2, 1976, pp. 76–91. For a comprehensive literary and bibliographical introduction see Davis, *The Drapier's Letters to the People of Ireland* (Oxford, 1935; rev. bibliography, 1965).
2. See *Corr*, III, p. 5.
3. See Swift's letter to Cartaret, ibid., pp. 11–13. Also Ferguson, *Jonathan Swift and Ireland*, p. 96, and Ehrenpreis, III, p. 207.
4. *Corr*, III, pp. 9–10.
5. *PW*, X, p. 61.
6. *Corr*, III, p. 12.
7. See Ehrenpreis' witty analysis of this relationship, op. cit., pp. 223–5.
8. *PW*, X, p. 29.
9. Ibid., p. 63.
10. Ibid.
11. The text of the proclamation is reprinted in *PW*, III, p. 205.
12. Quoted in Ferguson, *Jonathan Swift and Ireland*, p. 123.

13.   Although *To Middleton* was the fifth letter to be written, it was the sixth to be published, in 1735 by Faulkner in the *Works*. By the same logic, *To Molesworth*, the next to be printed after *To the Whole People of Ireland*, is conventionally referred to as the 'fifth' letter.

14.   *PW*, X, p. 107.

15.   Ibid., p. 86.

16.   Ibid., p. 127.

17.   *Corr*, III, p. 93. The reference to 'she' indicates Sarah Harding, who had taken over the business after her husband's death in April.

18.   See Ehrenpreis, III, p. 208, who also points out the importance of this figure in that part of *Gulliver's Travels* written in the spring of 1724, when Swift began the *Letters*.

19.   *PW*, X, p. 48.

20.   Ibid., p. 71.

21.   Ibid., p. 89.

22.   *PW*, IX, p. 236.

23.   See *Poems*, I, pp. 331–54.

24.   Reprinted in *PW*, X, pp. 145–9.

25.   See Ferguson, *Jonathan Swift and Ireland*, p. 111.

26.   Ehrenpreis, III, p. 317, for several of the following details.

27.   *Corr*, III, p. 87.

28.   Ibid., p. 89.

29.   See ibid., p. 102ff., for Swift's earliest comments on the purpose of his *Travels*.

30.   See Swift's letter of 7 July 1726 to a friend in Dublin, Thomas Tickell, in which the author says that the original manuscript could not be found 'without searching nine Houses and then sending to me the Key'. The same point is made the next day to Sheridan. See *Corr*, III, p. 138 and pp. 139–40.

31.   'An Unpublished Letter from Swift', Paul V. Thompson, in *The Library*, 5th ser., XXIII (1967) pp. 57–66. Here quoted from Ehrenpreis, III, p. 486.

32.   *Corr*, III, p. 140.

33.   Ibid., p. 153.

34.   Ehrenpreis, III, p. 329.

35.   See H. Williams, *Dean Swift's Library*, pp. 88–93.

36.   *PW*, XI, p. 199.

37.   *Corr*, III, p. 179.

38.   Ibid., p. 181.

39.   Ibid., p. 182.

40.   For a detailed account of the publishing history of the *Travels* see H. Williams' introduction to *Gulliver's Travels* (London, 1926). See also his introduction to *PW*, XI, pp. ix–xxviii.

41.   *Corr*, III, pp. 189–90.

42.   This section, from Chapter 3, was never published in Swift's lifetime, not even in Faulkner. Davis' edition, based on Faulkner, also excludes it. It was first printed in an 1899 London edition by G. R. Dennis.

43. See Williams' introduction to *PW*, XI, for most of the following detail.
44. A full and fascinating account of this text may be read in David Wooley's 'Swift's Copy of *Gulliver's Travels*', in *The Art of Jonathan Swift*, edited by Clive T. Probyn (London, 1978) pp. 131–78.
45. *Corr*, III, p. 198.
46. It was finally published, in front of the text, in Faulkner's 1735 edition.
47. *Corr*, III, p. 217.
48. Ibid., p. 226.
49. Ibid., p. 236.
50. See *PW*, V, pp. 201–8.
51. *Poems*, II, p. 421.

Chapter 6

1.   'On the Death of Mrs Johnson' in *PW*, V, pp. 227–36. This tribute was first published in 1765 by Deane Swift in his *Works*.
2.   Ibid., p. 231.
3.   Irvin Ehrenpreis, *Swift: The Man, His Work, and The Age*, III, *Dean Swift*, p. 549.
4.   *Corr*, III, pp. 257–8.
5.   Ibid., p. 260–3.
6.   *The Beggar's Opera* was first performed on 29 January 1728, shortly after this letter was written.
7.   *Corr*, III, pp. 263–4.
8.   *Corr*, IV, pp. 29–32.
9.   *PW*, XII, p. 8.
10. In *Some Observations*, the third of the *Drapier's Letters*.
11. *Corr*, III, pp. 280–3. After this appeal, Swift dropped Browne's name for all future editions.
12. *PW*, XII, p. 23.
13. Ibid., p. 23. See Davis' Introduction to this volume for details of Swift's contributions and the paper's publishing history, pp. xiv–xvii.
14. Ibid., p. 37.
15. *Corr*, III, p. 278.
16. For details of how Swift came to know the Achesons, and of the poems he wrote during his visits, see *Poems*, III, p. 845–908. Swift used Sir Arthur Acheson as the persona for one of his *Intelligencer* essays, no. XIX, 'a Country Gentleman in the North of Ireland' who addresses the Drapier on the nation's ruinous economy. See *PW*, XII, pp. 54–61.
17. *Poems*, III, pp. 855–6.
18. See *Poems*, II, pp. 443–53. In March 1729, writing to Pope, Swift says he tried to get the poem printed in the *Intelligencer*, but instead had it printed separately, which resulted in it being 'horribly mangled in the press'. See *Corr*, III, p. 314.

19. *Poems*, III, p. 875.
20. Ibid., p. 900.
21. *Corr*, III, pp. 311–12.
22. Ibid., pp. 330–1.
23. Ibid.
24. Ibid., p. 303.
25. Ibid., pp. 362–3.
26. See, for example, his letter to Pope, 13 February 1729, *Corr*, III, pp. 313–14.
27. Ibid., p. 373.
28. Ibid., pp. 386–7.
29. See Ferguson's chapter on these final tracts, in *Jonathan Swift and Ireland*, pp. 139–68.
30. *Corr*, III, p. 329.
31. 'The Irony of Swift', in *The Common Pursuit* (London, 1952) pp. 73–87.
32. *PW*, XII, p. 65.
33. Ibid., p. 80.
34. Ibid., p. 122.
35. Ibid., pp. 80–1.
36. Ibid., pp. 93–105.
37. See Ferguson, *Jonathan Swift and Ireland*, p. 171, for details of how the *Proposal* was advertised in the Dublin press.
38. See ibid., pp. 177–80, for background to events.
39. *Corr*, III, p. 434.
40. He enjoyed the Christmas season in the newly found company of his young cousin, Martha Whiteway, the Pilkingtons, the Grattans, and Delany. See Ehrenpreis, III, pp. 685–8.
41. In a letter to Lord Bathurst, *Corr*, III, p. 474.
42. In a letter to Countess of Suffolk, ibid., pp. 500–1.
43. Ibid., p. 493.
44. *Corr*, IV, p. 31.
45. *Corr*, III, p. 506.
46. For the complicated history of both versions see *Poems*, II, pp. 541–3, pp. 551–3, and Ehrenpreis, III, pp. 708–13.
47. *Poems*, III, p. 550.
48. *Corr*, III, p. 354.

Chapter 7

1. See Ferguson, *Jonathan Swift and Ireland*, pp. 181–4.
2. See *PW*, XIII, pp. 69–70 and 79–85.
3. Ibid., p. 82.
4. See Introduction, ibid., pp. xxv–xxvii.
5. For example *Some Reasons Against the Bill for Settling the Tythe of Hemp by a Modus* (1734), and *Speech on Lowering the Coin* (1736), *PW*, XIII, pp. 93–108 and pp. 117–20.
6. See *Observations Occasioned by Reading a Paper, Entitled The Case of the Woolen Manufacturers etc* (1733), and *Letter to the Printer of Thoughts on*

the Tillage of Ireland (1737), *PW*, XIII, pp. 87–92 and p. 143.

7. Ibid., p. 140.
8. Probably the most controversial dimension of Swift's literary character. For a critical overview, see H. Real and H. Vienken, ' "Those odious common Whores of which this Town is full": Swift's *A Beautiful Young Nymph Going to Bed*', *Arbeiten aus Anglislik und Amerikanistik*, 6, 1981, pp. 241–59.
9. See *Poems*, II, pp. 524–5 for details.
10. Ibid., p. 530.
11. See *PW*, V, pp. 337–40.
12. *Poems*, II, pp. 580–97.
13. Irvin Ehrenpreis, *Swift: The Man, His Works, and The Age*, III, *Dean Swift*, pp. 690–1.
14. *Poems*, III, p. 591.
15. For full contextual details see *Poems*, III, pp. 827–9.
16. Ibid., p. 831.
17. *PW*, IV, p. 118.
18. *Corr*, V, p. 172.
19. Ibid., p. 188.
20. For an account of Faulkner's career, see R. Ward, *Prince of Dublin Printers: The Letters of George Faulkner* (Kentucky, 1972).
21. See Swift's letters to Pope and Motte in June/July 1732, *Corr*, IV, pp. 29–32 and 41–3.
22. Ibid., p. 154.
23. Ibid., pp. 197–8.
24. Ibid., p. 202.
25. In his *Preface* to the 1763 edition. See *PW*, XIII, pp. 201–7.
26. *Corr*, IV, p. 304.
27. Ibid., pp. 370–4.
28. Ibid., p. 494.
29. Vols V and VI appeared in 1738, Vol. VII in 1741.
30. For details see Ward, *Prince of Dublin Printers*, pp. 24–31.
31. *Corr*, IV, p. 382.
32. Ibid., p. 344.
33. See Swift's letter to Pope explaining the transaction, *Corr* V, pp. 57–9.
34. See his accompanying letter to Swift, ibid., pp. 184–5.
35. See Williams' notes, *Corr*, IV, pp. 382–5.
36. Ibid., pp. 416–18.
37. Ibid., p. 300.
38. For the text, see *PW*, XIII, pp. 149–57.
39. *Corr*, V, p. 192.
40. *Poems*, III, p. 843. Not all editors accept the authenticity of either the tale or the poem. If both are fictions, they are perfectly in sympathy with the spirit of Swift.

Index